Ending the US War in Afghanistan

Ending the US War in Afghanistan

A Primer

by David Wildman and Phyllis Bennis

OLIVE
BRANCH
PRESS

An imprint of Interlink Publishing Group, Inc.
www.interlinkbooks.com

First published in 2010 by

OLIVE BRANCH PRESS
An imprint of Interlink Publishing Group, Inc.
46 Crosby Street, Northampton, Massachusetts 01060
www.interlinkbooks.com

Library of Congress Cataloging-in-Publication Data
Wildman, David.
Ending the US war in Afghanistan : a primer / by David Wildman
and Phyllis Bennis.—1st American ed.
p. cm.
Includes bibliographical references.
ISBN 978-1-56656-785-5 (pbk.)
1. Afghan War, 2001—Causes. 2. Afghan War, 2001—United States.
3. United States—Armed Forces—Afghanistan. 4. Afghan War,
2001—Influence. 5. Afghan War, 2001—Peace. 6. Disengagement
(Military science) I. Bennis, Phyllis, 1951– II. Title. III. Title: Ending
the U.S. war in Afghanistan.
DS371.412.W55 2009
958.104'7—dc22

2009043874

Book design by Juliana Spear
Cover image: Afghan children look at U.S. soldiers establishing a base in Kandaksai,
Afghanistan, along the Pakistan border. (AP Photo/B.K.Bangash)

Printed and bound in the United States of America
10 9 8 7 6 5 4 3 2 1

To request our complete 40-page full-color catalog,
please call us toll free at 1-800-238-LINK, visit our website at
www.interlinkbooks.com or write to Interlink Publishing
46 Crosby Street, Northampton, MA 01060

*When two bulls fight, it is the shrubs
and plants that suffer.*

—Afghan proverb

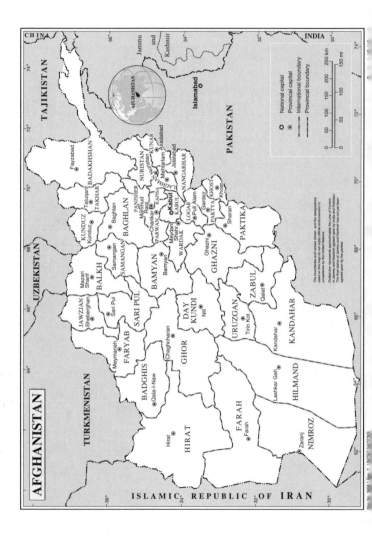

FACTS AND FIGURES:
ISLAMIC REPUBLIC OF AFGHANISTAN

GEOGRAPHY

Area: 251,825 sq mi/647,500 sq km (slightly smaller than Texas), divided into 34 provinces

Climate: arid to semiarid; cold winters and hot summers

Terrain: landlocked; mostly rugged mountains; plains in north and southwest; the Hindu Kush mountains that run northeast to southwest divide the northern provinces from the rest of the country

Natural resources: natural gas, petroleum, coal, copper, chromite, talc, barites, sulfur, lead, zinc, iron ore, salt, precious and semiprecious stones

Environmental challenges: limited natural fresh water resources; inadequate supplies of potable water; soil degradation; overgrazing; deforestation (much of the remaining forests are being cut down for fuel and building materials); desertification; air and water pollution

PEOPLE

Population: 33,609,937 (July 2009 est.)

Median age: 17.6 years

Total fertility rate: 6.53 children born per woman (2009 est.; fourth highest in the world)

Urbanization: 24% of total population lives in urban areas (2008)

Ethnic groups: Pashtun 42%, Tajik 27%, Hazara 9%, Uzbek 9%, Aimak 4%, Turkmen 3%, Baloch 2%, other 4%

Religions: Sunni Muslim 80%, Shia Muslim 19%, other 1%

Languages: Afghan Persian or Dari (official) 50%, Pashto (official) 35%, Turkic languages (primarily Uzbek and Turkmen) 11%, 30 minor languages (primarily Balochi and Pashai) 4%, much bilingualism

DEVELOPMENT

Literacy (age 15 and over can read and write): total population 28.1%; male 43.1%; female 12.6% (2000 est.)

Life expectancy at birth: 44.64 years (212th lowest in the world)

Infant mortality rate: 151.95 deaths/1,000 live births (third highest in the world)

Population below poverty line: 53% (2003)

ECONOMY

GDP, per capita (PPP): $800 (2008 est.; 215th lowest in the world)

GDP and composition of workforce by sector: agriculture: 31% (80% of labor force); industry: 26% (10% of labor force); services: 43% (10% of labor force) (2004 est.)

Unemployment rate (official): 40%

Agriculture—products: opium, wheat, fruits, nuts; wool, mutton, sheepskins, lambskins

Industries: small-scale production of textiles, soap, furniture, shoes, fertilizer, cement; handwoven carpets; natural gas, coal, copper

Source: Central Intelligence Agency, *World Factbook: Afghanistan* www.cia.gov/library/publications/the-world-factbook/geos/AF.html> accessed 20 July 2009.

HISTORICAL TIMELINE

3000–2000 BCE—Ancient land of what is now Afghanistan becomes an important crossroads in Asia between Mesopotamia and civilizations to the east.

2000–1500 BCE—Aryan tribes from Central Asia establish roots in the area.

600 BCE—Zoroastrianism, one of the first religions in recorded history and one of the first monotheistic religions, takes hold in Afghanistan.

600–500 BCE—Persian Empire takes over Afghanistan region.

330 BCE—Alexander the Great defeats Persians, giving Macedonians control of modern Afghanistan.

100 CE—Indo-European Kushans win control of Afghan region and spread Buddhism to the area.

600–700 CE—Invading Arab armies first introduce Islam to Afghanistan region.

1219—Genghis Khan leads Mongol takeover of the region.

1370—Tamerlane invades the region.

1747—Afghanistan created as a single country under Ahmed Shah Durrani.

1747–19th century—The "Great Game": Britain and Russia compete for influence in Central Asia. Russian southward expansion worries British Empire, where strategists disagree, some favoring a push to try to conquer Afghanistan and some seeing Afghanistan as a neutral buffer state protecting India, the "jewel of the British Crown," from Russian influence.

1826—Dost Mohammed Khan takes Kabul and rules Afghanistan until he is toppled by the British during the first Anglo–Afghan War.

1839–1842—First Anglo–Afghan War: British army flees after three years, deterred by the rising costs of occupation, constant uprisings, and their underestimation of the Afghan army.

1878—Sher Ali rejects a British mission to Kabul after having granted the same privilege to Russia, sparking the second Anglo–Afghan War. After a successful invasion, Britain establishes a protectorate, instating Abdur Rahman as amir, while remaining in control of Afghan foreign policy.

1893—British establish highly contested Durand Line as Afghan–Indian border.

1880–1901—Amir Abdur Rahman forcefully suppresses internal rebellions, raises taxes, and establishes provincial governors, successfully unifying the Afghan state under one law and one rule.

1919—Third Anglo–Afghan War; peace treaty recognizes Afghanistan's independence, including agency over foreign policy.

1929—Amanullah Khan abdicates and is forced into exile by revolts following Western-style modernization reforms.

1945—Afghanistan joins United Nations.

1947—Pakistan is carved out of Indian and Afghan lands as Britain withdraws from India.

1953—Mohammad Daoud becomes prime minister, receives military aid from USSR, introduces liberal measures for the status of women (purdah abolished, universities become coeducational, right to work).

1964—Afghanistan adopts new constitution, becomes constitutional monarchy.

1973—Mohammad Daoud overthrows king, proclaims republic and instates himself as president; outcry from both leftists and conservatives.

1978—Daoud overthrown and killed. Cofounder of Afghan Communist Party Nur Mohammed Taraki becomes president. Mujahideen movement is born as traditionalist rebels object to social reforms.

1979—US ambassador killed, US suspends assistance. President Taraki assassinated, Hafizullah Amin takes presidency. USSR invades in December, Amin and followers executed. Deputy Prime Minister Babrak Karmal becomes president. US-backed Mujahideen unite against Soviet and Afghan armies.

1979–1988—Afghanistan is a cold war battleground. US, Pakistan, China, Iran, and Saudi Arabia send money and arms to Mujahideen (notably Stinger Missiles to shoot down Soviet helicopters) while USSR maintains more than 100,000 soldiers and backs President Karmal (who is replaced by Mohammed Najibullah, former head of secret police, in 1986). Half the population is displaced. In 1985, Gorbachev pledges to withdraw troops, leading to Geneva Peace Accords. But civil war continues, as Mujahideen continue to fight "Soviet puppet government."

1992—Mujahideen take Kabul; Najibullah overthrown. An Islamic state is proclaimed, and Professor Burhannudin Rabbani is elected president. Two years later, a faction of Mujahideen form the Taliban militia, challenging the Rabbani government. Civil war continues.

1996—The Taliban take Kabul. Rabbani flees to join the Northern Alliance, led by Massoud and Dostum. Islamic law is strictly enforced.

1998—After bombings of US embassies in Africa, US launches cruise missiles on Khost region, aiming at al-Qaeda's training camps.

1999–2001—UN sanctions against the Taliban for their offering sanctuary to terrorist groups.

September 11, 2001—Hijackers crash four commercial airliners in the US, two into the World Trade Center in New York City, one into the Pentagon, and one that is brought down by passengers in a field in Pennsylvania; it is believed that Osama bin Laden, thought to be hiding in Afghanistan, organized the attacks for al-Qaeda.

October 7, 2001—US and British forces begin air strikes on Afghanistan.

December 7, 2001—Taliban abandon last stronghold in Kandahar.

December 22, 2001—Hamid Karzai sworn in as interim president of Afghanistan.

June 13, 2002—Hamid Karzai elected by loya jirga; will serve until first national election.

August 11, 2003—NATO takes over security operations in Kabul.

January 4, 2004—Afghanistan's constitution approved by loya jirga.

October 9, 2004—In the first popular election under the new constitution, Hamid Karzai becomes president.

September 18, 2005—First parliamentary and provincial elections under new constitution; parliament convenes in December.

2006—NATO takes control of southern and eastern regions of Afghanistan from US forces.

February–March 2009—US President Barack Obama approves sending an additional 17,000 troops, then 4,000 more, to Afghanistan.

2009—By November, US casualties in Afghanistan under Obama (288) rise to more than double previous two years; almost 30 percent of total post-2001 US military injuries occur between July and November. On December 1st Obama announced an escalation of 30,000 troops at an additional cost of at least $30 billion.

—PART I—

The US War in Afghanistan

Is the US war in Afghanistan a "good war"?

Just days after September 11, 2001, before the US war in Afghanistan began, a *Los Angeles Times* reporter wrote from the sun-baked, crowded refugee camps in Pakistan whose populations were expanding every hour with desperate Afghans fleeing the war they knew was coming. He posed a critical challenge: "As the US embarks on its global hunt for terrorists," he said, "Afghanistan looms as a crucial early test of whether America will be able to defeat elusive enemies without declaring war on an entire people."[1] The US failed the test. The US war in Afghanistan has not been able to bring to justice those responsible for September 11, and it almost immediately became a quagmire.

The assault on Afghanistan began on October 7, 2001. Immediately after the attacks on September 11, the administration of George W. Bush had announced its intention to go to war in response. The bombardment, covert operations, and later invasion of Afghanistan would constitute the first strike in what was quickly called the "global war on terror"—an expanding war without borders, without limits, potentially without end. While longstanding strategic and geopolitical interests had motivated previous US attempts to control Afghanistan (as so many earlier empires had tried to do), Bush's war would now be sold as an act of legal, legitimate, even praiseworthy vengeance, aimed at going after those responsible for 9/11.

It was an illusion driven by fear: that a full-scale conventional war—an all-out air assault followed by a massive invasion of ground troops that quickly overthrew the government and occupied much of the country—would soon find and bring to justice Osama bin Laden and other top al-Qaeda and Taliban figures. Somehow the war was also going to result in a peaceful, unified, secular Afghan democracy, where all children went to school, farmers grew wheat instead of opium poppies, women were equal, pro-Western governments were peacefully elected, and US troops were welcomed as liberators.

Just a few months after the war began, the fantasy began to crumble. A *San Francisco Chronicle* columnist asked plaintively, "Who hijacked our war?" What happened, he asked, to "that gutsy war of bringing the World Trade Center and Pentagon killers to justice?"[2] But the war in Afghanistan had never been "gutsy," and had never been about justice. Certainly the lofty goals of democratization, "liberating" women, and bringing modernity and wealth to Afghanistan had never been close to being met. And the failure to meet those goals was not because the war in Afghanistan so quickly morphed into the illegal invasion and occupation of Iraq a year and a half later.

Certainly revenge against those linked to the

perpetrators of 9/11 was one of the reasons for the war. But as Michael Kinsley noted in the online magazine *Slate*,

> starting with overwhelming approval for retribution against the perpetrators of 9/11, [the Bush administration] has nudged us down the slippery slope from destroying al-Qaeda head-quarters to destroying the government that "harbored" the headquarters, to invading or bombing other countries where al-Qaeda may have operations, or that sponsor al-Qaeda oper-ations elsewhere, to military action against countries that harbor or sponsor terrorists unconn-ected to 9/11, to action against countries that do other bad things, like developing nuclear weapons.[3]

The attacks of September 11 were a horrific crime. If the US were to remain a country ruled by law, the response would have been to engage the world in a cooperative effort to find those who had committed this crime and bring them to face international justice, empowering organizations such as the United Nations and the International Criminal Court. The US would have launched an immediate, intensive investigation into the root causes of how such an attack could occur and even why people in many parts of the world had sympathized with those who committed it. Perhaps most importantly, the US would have made sure that its response did not result in greater suffering and more deaths.

But the US did none of these things. Instead it launched a war of vengeance in Afghanistan, the first campaign of the "global war on terror." And that war has failed to bring justice and failed to make anyone safer.

Previous US decisions to respond militarily to terrorist attacks have all failed for the same reasons. One, they have all killed, injured, or rendered even more desperate already-impoverished innocents. Two, they haven't worked to stop terrorism. In 1986 Ronald Reagan ordered the bombing of Tripoli and Benghazi to punish Libyan leader Muammar Ghadafi for an explosion in a discotheque in Germany that had killed two GIs. Ghadafi survived, but several dozen Libyan civilians, including Ghadafi's three-year-old daughter, were killed. Just a couple years later came the Lockerbie disaster, for which Libya would take responsibility. In 1999, in response to the attacks on US embassies in Kenya and Tanzania, US bombers attacked Osama bin Laden's training camps in Afghanistan and an allegedly bin Laden–linked pharmaceutical factory in the Sudan. It turned out the Sudanese factory had no connection to bin Laden, but the US attack had destroyed the only producer of vital vaccines for children growing up in the profound scarcity of central Africa. And the assault on the camps in the Afghan mountains clearly did not prevent the attacks of September 11, 2001.

Even more important than the fact that the US war on Afghanistan has failed to stop terrorism has been the war's terrible consequences for the people of Afghanistan. It could not have been a surprise to the Bush administration and Pentagon officials that US military strikes in Afghanistan would cause devastation. Less than a week after the 9/11 attacks, the likely result of the looming Afghan war was already clear. The *Los Angeles Times* described how

> aid workers fear that a major US offensive could trigger mass starvation in a land where millions are already suffering. With hundreds of thousands of Afghan refugees already on the move, food supplies in their nation running out and winter just weeks away, US military action against Afghanistan could lead to mass starvation, aid agencies warned Sunday. The UN refugee agency estimated that by Saturday as many as 300,000 Afghans had fled the southeastern city of Kandahar, the ruling Taliban movement's spiritual capital and a presumed target of any airstrikes in retaliation for last week's terrorist attacks in the United States. "That means up to half the city's population has already left, more are following, and the mass exodus is spreading across the country as refugees head toward Iran and Pakistan," said Yousaf Hassan, a senior official in Islamabad, the Pakistani capital, with the Office of the U.N. High Commissioner for Refugees.... "We're talking about a huge catastrophe in the making," said Andrew Wilder, field office director

of the nonprofit agency Save the Children's $6-million aid program for Afghans.[4]

That huge catastrophe soon happened. The bombing and invasion of Afghanistan was not a "good" war, or even a good idea. Congresswoman Barbara Lee—currently chair of the Congressional Black Caucus—was right when she stood alone in Congress, just after the 9/11 attacks, to cast the sole, brave, and prophetic vote against authorizing the Bush administration to go to war.

Nor has the war on Afghanistan become a "good"—or even a better—war since President Barack Obama was sworn into office. President Obama himself said, "I'm absolutely convinced that you cannot solve the problem of Afghanistan, the Taliban, and the spread of extremism in the region solely through military means. We're going to have to use diplomacy, we're going to have to use development."[5] Military leaders from NATO to the Pentagon have already acknowledged that there is no military solution. Researchers at the Carnegie Endowment for International Peace found that "the only meaningful way to halt the insurgency's momentum is to start withdrawing troops. The presence of foreign troops is the most important element driving the resurgence of the Taliban."[6] The Afghanistan war was and remains illegal, immoral, and ineffective as a response to the crimes of September 11.

By August 2009, a majority of the US people had come to understand this. A national CNN poll demonstrated that 54 percent opposed the US war against the Taliban and al-Qaeda, and only 41 percent supported it.[7] By September 2009, the *Wall Street Journal* was reporting that 38 percent of people in the US supported an immediate and orderly withdrawal from Afghanistan.[8]

What does the war look like on the ground?

The situation on the ground eight years after the US invasion is deteriorating for civilians and armed forces alike. There is a basic formula in Afghanistan over the past 30 years of war that remains true today: the more guns there are—no matter in whose hands—the more civilian deaths. Each escalation of US, coalition, or Afghan military forces or armed opposition groups introduces more arms, with invariably more casualties and more destruction of infrastructure.

Day to day, the war in Afghanistan is much more low-tech than in Iraq, and its impact varies widely from one community to another. The Taliban and other armed opposition groups use only light, portable weapons (rifles, rocket-propelled grenades, mortars, homemade bombs), cell phones, and light vehicles. The US and coalition forces have jet fighter-bombers with guided missiles, helicopters, armored personnel carriers, personal body armor, and many more high-tech, powerful, and lethal weapons. The cost for insurgents to fight is in the low millions, while the cost for the US is in the hundreds of billions. Despite this disparity of resources, the Taliban are now widely seen as winning.

The nature of asymmetrical guerilla and counterinsurgency warfare was captured in an exchange between Senator Lindsay Graham and Admiral Mike Mullen, head of the Joint Chiefs of Staff. After Mullen acknowledged that the Taliban have no tanks and no planes, Senator Graham asked why then were they doing so well. Mullen replied, "They've watched us. They're very good at it. It's their country."[9]

As in any counterinsurgency war, in Afghanistan when large numbers of troops enter an area, as the US did in Helmand in the summer of 2009, the Taliban lay low, move to target another area, and plant more IEDs at night. The period from July through November 2009 saw the highest US casualty rates since the 2001 invasion. Many of the casualties were not actually in Helmand, where 4,000 Marines and 400 Afghan soldiers had swarmed in, but from attacks in neighboring provinces.

For US troops, much of the time the war is defined by a stressful mix of anxiety and boredom— being out on patrols in crowded city streets or remote mountain valleys and waiting for things to happen. The greatest fear and greatest source of US casualties are improvised explosive devices (IEDs). In November 2009 there were 68,000 US forces and over 71,000 private contractors working for the Department of Defense, and additional security contractors with USAID and the State Department. As the number of coalition forces has steadily increased since 2002, so have the challenges to the long and vulnerable US supply lines running through remote areas of Pakistan. Military supply trucks are daily subject to attacks that make these few paved roads into Afghanistan more dangerous for everyone.

US forces deployed in rural areas call for constant air backup from fighter jets, bombers, drones, and helicopters. US air superiority and re-supply operations are increasingly dependent on support from Afghanistan's neighbors. In addition to the Bagram airbase in Afghanistan, the US relies heavily on an airbase in nearby Kyrgyzstan. When the Kyrgyz government demanded the US leave the country, negotiations resulted in the rent the US paid for the airbase tripling.

In cities, the Taliban target foreign troops, Afghan government officials, and Afghans who work with internationals. Since most internationals are in cities, that is also where they are most vulnerable to kidnappings.

For coalition forces operating outside cities, IEDs are one of the greatest threats. For Afghan civilians, US air strikes are a major source of casualties, as well as armed groups' and Taliban attacks on coalition forces and government officials in public places. The continual possibility of another attack leaves Afghans and NGOs operating in Afghanistan in constant fear. In some sense, Afghans felt more secure when the Taliban were in power, when there were repressive religious rules, especially for women, but almost no random criminal violence. Now the military attacks and greater insecurity have led to widespread crime and violence, such as kidnappings for ransom.

The US is also increasingly using humanitarian aid as a political weapon to enhance its military action. As the US seeks to expand civil–military cooperation through Pentagon-directed provincial reconstruction teams and other means, it escalates the risks to aid workers (both Afghan and international) who are then seen as working in support of the US and the corrupt Kabul government.

Some of the most intense fighting in the past few years has been in an isolated valley in Kunar province, which is right on the Pakistan border in eastern Afghanistan. The US has used a "persistent presence" strategy of placing a number of small outposts in remote valleys rather than near population centers. The remote valleys of Kunar, Nuristan, and other parts of Laghman (all east of Kabul) have a longstanding tradition of fundamentalism and suspicion of all outsiders. By one estimate, close to 20 percent of all fighting in Afghanistan has taken place in Kunar province and 75 percent of all bombs dropped have landed there. Precisely because US outposts are so isolated, the US military repeatedly calls in air strikes, which further anger the whole population. One study of the area concludes, "the presence of US forces exacerbates tensions and results in anger and resentment. This facilitates violence in the region, rather than stability and security."[10]

Governors, who are appointed by the president in Kabul rather than elected, are often seen as corrupt outsiders by rural communities. In another valley, US forces worked with the local governor to threaten communities with sanctions. The governor threatened to cut off subsistence farmers' access to tea, sugar, and cooking oil if they did not join sides with the governor and US military.[11] Such instances of collective punishment raise questions about whether "protecting the people" is really another way of controlling communities by forcing them to rely on US protection. While the US claims its mission is to protect the people and strengthen ties between communities and the government, its military actions undermine its stated goal.

What do Afghans think about the war and the role of the US and NATO?

Historians have described Afghanistan as the "graveyard of empires." Alexander the Great and Genghis Khan came with powerful armies; they soon left. In the nineteenth century, British and Russian militaries repeatedly came, tried to conquer, and left. For ten years the Soviet military tried to rule; they left. Eight years have passed since the US military swept in and in a matter of weeks removed the Taliban from power. Today the number of US/NATO troops continues to rise, but the number of Afghan civilian casualties, the level of insecurity, corruption, and unmet development needs are all higher than ever.

One thing almost all Afghans do agree on, across the political spectrum, from diverse ethnic backgrounds and different geographic locations, is that the US and NATO, like all previous foreign military forces, should and will leave. The only questions are when and under what circumstances.

After the massive US bombing campaign in the fall of 2001, when a relatively small number of US special forces joined with Afghanistan's Northern Alliance coalition of largely Hazeri, Uzbek, and Tajik forces to remove the Pashtun-based Taliban from power, most Afghans were happy to see an end to the repressive rule of the Taliban. For a brief period, the initial US military footprint on the ground was relatively light. Yet as the US military presence continued to support the Northern Alliance and other armed groups—all of whom had human rights records almost as brutal as the Taliban's—in their effort to grab and solidify power in key government ministries and the army, popular resentment toward the US and NATO presence quickly grew.

Pashtun areas in the south and east of Afghanistan have born the brunt of CIA attacks, night raids, and air strikes, leading to much higher levels of civilian casualties. The number of civilian casualties has gone up each year since 2002, with over 2,100 killed in 2008. While more civilians have been killed by the Taliban and other armed opposition groups than by the US and its allies, there is a growing public outcry in Afghanistan against the escalating civilian deaths caused by US and NATO forces.

The US and other Western societies place considerable emphasis on public opinion polls as a measure of what people are thinking. Opinion polls in Afghanistan often rely on telephone access or survey-takers who are distrusted as outsiders in many communities, and so invariably miss significant portions of the population, thus telling at most part of the story and rarely portraying the range of opinions among different communities. But even with those limitations, it is still startling to see how consistently the polls have indicated opposition to the US-led military occupation. In February 2009, an ABC–BBC–ARD poll showed

> sagging support for US efforts in that country, with airstrikes a chief concern. A quarter of the Afghans polled said that attacks on American or allied forces are justifiable, double the proportion saying so in late 2006. The poll… also shows plummeting support for President Hamid Karzai and the Afghan government, and a sharp decline in the proportion of people who think the nation is heading in the right direction. …[R]atings of US forces have declined precipitously; 32 percent said US and coalition forces are performing well, down from 68 percent in 2005.[12]

The majority of Afghans in isolated rural areas get most of their news by word of mouth and radio. Each new incident in which civilians are killed by US/NATO forces is broadcast on the radio and fans popular resentment in many areas beyond the immediate community that was hit.

Most of the civilians killed by US/NATO forces have been hit by air strikes and drone strikes. These strikes are often based on faulty intelligence or occur when a US ground unit gets ambushed and air support is called in despite the civilians in the area. Besides the loss of life, the remoteness of air strikes—especially by unmanned drones—is deeply insulting to the Pashtun code of honor, or *pashtunwali*. Breaking into people's homes with night raids and killing women and children are also grave offenses of *pashtunwali*. Even some communities that oppose the Taliban have taken up armed resistance to US forces because such actions by foreigners demonstrate disrespect and dishonor for the community.

Afghanistan has never had a strong central government and most Afghans have little trust for centralized authority. Instead they have relied on the decentralized local leadership of shuras, or councils of village elders, who develop pragmatic and shifting alliances with one another. As the number of US and NATO troops steadily increased from 2002 to 2009, Afghans saw the occupation as an effort to create a strong centralized Afghan government with an Afghan national army, Afghan police, and various national ministries. Many Afghan communities see this top-down "nation-building" project as bypassing, or worse, deliberately undermining the longstanding authority of local shuras. The Karzai government, particularly after the election in 2009, which was widely viewed as deeply flawed with voter fraud, is seen as corrupt and lacking respect or authority anywhere outside Kabul. Since he was installed in power by the US-backed coalition, Afghanistan's Pashtun President Karzai has been derisively portrayed as the "mayor of Kabul." With parliament and government ministries filled with warlords and others demanding bribes from the local population, the national elections have had little meaning and little accountability to the needs of local communities. As a result, Pashtuns do not see Karzai as a legitimate representative or defender of their interests. Journalists and Afghanistan experts Paul Fitzgerald and Elizabeth Gould point out, "As long as the United States continues to legitimize Tajik, Uzbek and Hazara warlords at the expense of Pashtun goals, the Taliban will continue to be viewed by the injured Pashtun population as an army of national pride. Unless the West adapts to this local reality, it will lose."[13]

Local shuras offer greater space for grassroots participation and accountability in decision-making. Local leaders often align themselves with whatever regional forces they believe will be most likely to preserve their local autonomy. This in part explains why bitter enemies can sometimes shift to become close allies seemingly overnight.

Afghan resistance to foreign military power should not be construed as categorical distrust of foreigners or xenophobia. To the contrary, Afghan culture values an extravagant sense of hospitality. As a longstanding way station on the Silk Road, Afghan communities have welcomed foreign traders and travelers for centuries. In remote and isolated villages where the next town may be more than a day's journey away, hospitality to strangers becomes almost a moral obligation for mutual survival. If foreigners stop to have some tea and share stories—still the greatest source of outside news in rural areas—then they are welcome. Fitzgerald and Gould note the tragic contrast between today's reality and Afghan cultural history: "For thousands of years a hub for trade and a melting pot of cultures, Afghanistan is now the world's largest exporter of heroin, a culture of unbridled exploitation and the most radical and extreme forms of Islam."[14]

For 30 years the US has come to Afghanistan not to sit over tea, not to share stories or trade, but bringing guns and trying to impose its own political agenda at the expense of Afghan people and traditions. Since 1979 the US government has armed and supported some of the most brutal, corrupt warlords in Afghanistan (Gulbuddin Hekmatyar, Osama bin Laden). Billions of dollars in armaments, promises of reconstruction, and a surge in US troops have not improved the quality of life for most Afghans. British journalist David Loyn noted in 2009 that while US military tactics may not be as harsh as the Soviets' were, "as the military activity intensified, the effect on an Afghan farmer must have felt exactly the same as the war ebbed and flowed across his fields with no sign of an end."[15] It is not surprising that growing numbers of Afghans are saying to the US: stop sending arms, stop killing Afghan civilians, stop trying to protect us.

What does international law say about the US invasion and occupation?

The United States is bound by and accountable to international law, of which the United Nations Charter is the central core. Under the Charter, member states of the UN are prohibited from using military force for almost all purposes—including retaliation, vengeance, punishment, or preventing future attacks. The UN Security Council can collectively authorize the use of force to defend international peace and security, but an individual country can legally use military force only in self-defense.

Self-defense is defined in Article 51 of the UN Charter. The Bush administration argued that Article 51 authorized the US to use force against Afghanistan. But the Charter did not authorize the US invasion. The legal problem was that the attacks of September 11 were over quickly. During the attacks themselves, the US certainly had a legal right of self-defense, which might have meant scrambling a fighter jet to shoot down the second plane before it hit the second World Trade Center tower. But by that afternoon, after the planes went down and the attacks (though of course not the human aftermath) were over, there was no continuing attack to defend against—and since there was no evidence of another "imminent" attack, self-defense under Article 51 no longer applied.

Article 51's authority is quite limited. It authorizes the use of military force to defend against an existing attack, but only "until the Security Council has taken measures necessary" to deal with the problem. The US certainly would not have needed to go to the Council for permission if it had tried—with military force or otherwise—to stop the attacks while they were underway. But Article 51 required Security Council authorization for the use of military force once the actual attacks were over.

The US did indeed convene an emergency meeting of the Council within 24 hours of the September 11 attacks, and could have requested authorization at that time. But Washington specifically abjured from calling for Security Council or other UN authorization for military force. Instead, Council Resolution 1368, passed unanimously on September 12, did *not* authorize either UN, coalition, or unilateral US military action. It was not taken under the explicit authority of Chapter VII of the UN Charter, a requirement for any authorization of the use of military force. Absent that authorization, the unilateral US military invasion of Afghanistan weeks after the attacks in New York and Washington, launched across the world against uncertain targets of unproven connection to the perpetrators of 9/11, but with inevitable and disastrous civilian consequences, remains a violation of international law and the UN Charter.

Resolution 1368 "unequivocally condemns" the September 11 attacks, and expresses deepest sympathy to the victims and the people and government of the US. The resolution calls on "all States to work together urgently to bring to justice the perpetrators, organizers and sponsors of these terrorist attacks and stresses that those responsible for aiding, supporting or harboring the perpetrators, organizers and sponsors of these acts will be held accountable." It "calls also on the international community to redouble their efforts to prevent and suppress terrorist acts including by increased cooperation and full implementation of the relevant international anti-terrorist conventions and Security Council resolutions." The reference to the conventions is particularly significant since the US has refused to sign several of these anti-terror initiatives.

Crucially, the Council then "expresses its readiness to take all necessary steps to respond to the terrorist attacks of 11 September 2001, and to combat all forms of terrorism, in accordance with its responsibilities under the Charter of the United Nations; and [d]ecides to remain seized of the matter."

What the Council did not do is authorize any military force, a legal decision clarified further by the absence of a reference to Chapter VII, and the crucial concluding language that the Council "remains seized" of the issue. In UN diplo-speak, that means the issue remains on the Council's agenda, and under the Council's jurisdiction, to be revisited as necessary.

In an October 2001 analysis of the international law factors involved in the US military response to the September 11 attacks, the legal director of the British human rights organization INTERIGHTS described how

> self-defense under the Charter... is clearly permissible only as a temporary measure pending Security Council engagement. If measures of force are initially justified, as necessary and proportionate self-defense, they may still fall foul of the law if they are coupled with a subsequent failure to engage the Security Council.[16]

In other words, even if an initial military attack in the name of self-defense had been deemed lawful, the US would still be in violation if it later refused to return to the Council for discussion, involvement, and approval for further action.

In fact, the somewhat creative US claim of what Bush's legal supporters called "preventive self-defense" is a concept not included within the UN Charter or international law. Article 51 was deliberately kept narrow, so that the claim of "self-defense" could not be used arbitrarily or out of convenience. An invasion of Afghanistan weeks after an attack that was carried out by nationals of countries other than Afghanistan does not fall within the deliberately restrictive confines of the legal use of military force.

Because the US invasion and occupation of Afghanistan did not comply with the requirements of the UN Charter, the US congressional resolution passed a few days after September 11, which authorized the president to use force against the perpetrators of the attack, is itself a violation of international law. The claim that the war in Afghanistan was legal because Congress said it was ignores the reality that no act of parliament or government, including that of the US Congress, can legalize an act of war prohibited by international law.

What are the human and economic costs of the war?

Afghanistan has been at war for 30 years. From the time of the CIA intervention and Soviet invasion of 1979 until the present, war, occupation, insecurity, and poverty have shaped Afghan lives and Afghanistan as a country. In the US, the majority of press coverage and discussion among the political elite focuses on US, and to a lesser degree NATO and other international military, casualties. The mainstream press in the US has occasionally shown concern regarding the impact of rising Afghan civilian casualties on US and/or Afghan public support for the war, but little attention has been paid to the casualties themselves. Thus the extent of, and more importantly, the consistent rise in civilian deaths, has rarely been discussed.

International organizations have been monitoring civilian casualties in Afghanistan only since 2006; the total documented from that time through September 2009 is 6,517.[17] In 2008, during the last year of the Bush administration, the United Nations mission in Afghanistan documented a 40 percent rise in civilian casualties from 2007, with a total of 2,118 people killed. The UN report acknowledged new US and NATO "policies and procedures to minimise the impact of their operations on civilians... [b]ut US, NATO and Afghan operations also have led to [a] rise in civilian casualties."[18]

When Barack Obama took office as president the following year, he announced additional shifts in policy in Afghanistan aimed at making the protection of Afghan civilians the highest priority. But by August 2009, a new UN report had been released that documented another rise in civilians killed in Afghanistan, "with bombings by insurgents and air strikes by international forces the biggest killers." The report "warned that more civilians would likely be killed as insurgents try to battle a troop increase by the US administration." The UN recognized again that the US and its allies had made it a priority to minimize civilian casualties, but said that despite this effort the US, NATO, and the Afghan government were responsible for the deaths of more than one-third of the civilians killed in just the first eight months of 2009, mostly by air strikes. The total number of civilian deaths was 24 percent higher than the total in 2008, and 48 percent higher than in 2007. Ominously, the report also noted that throughout those first eight months of 2009, the number of civilian deaths had risen every month but February, the height of the Afghan winter.[19]

It is clear that civilian deaths result from foreign troops' presence in their communities. The Taliban's violence has been brutal and repressive, but not arbitrary; civilians killed in insurgent attacks on Afghan government buildings, marketplaces, or on the roads, are almost always the victim of attacks aimed specifically at US or NATO (or sometimes US-backed Afghan government) troops. Since civilians don't have access to body armor or armored personnel carriers, the civilian toll will always be higher than the military toll. When the foreign troops are removed, there will be fewer insurgent attacks and thus fewer casualties among local civilians.

US and NATO air strikes have been particularly lethal for Afghanistan's civilians. A Human Rights Watch report in September 2009 that examined the impact of air strikes on Afghan civilians found that almost all the resulting deaths came from air strikes called in by troops on the ground having problems—a phenomenon likely to escalate with increases in US troops. One HRW representative noted, "Mistakes by the US and NATO have dramatically decreased public support for the Afghan government and the presence of international forces providing security to Afghans."[20]

Similarly, public support for the war is also decreasing in those countries providing troops in Afghanistan. A US air strike called in by German soldiers in Kunduz province in early September 2009 resulted in the deaths of scores of civilians. With German public opinion already strongly against the war, and many Germans mistakenly believing that the 4,000 German troops serving in the NATO force were only working in recon-struction, the air strike led to increased domestic pressure on the German government to bring its troops home. This incident also challenged the restoration of close ties between the US and Germany (and potentially other allies) that the election of President Obama had made possible.[21]

The escalation in fighting in Afghanistan that began in 2006 also led to increased military casualties among US, NATO, and other allied troops. By November 2009, 918 US troops had died in the Afghanistan war, along with 597 from allied countries (the largest contingents by far being the

217 Britons and 131 Canadians).[22] Of those US and allied deaths over eight years, 20 percent occurred just from July through mid-November 2009.

The number of injured Afghan civilians is difficult, even impossible, to ascertain. There are certainly extensive physical injuries from IEDs, bombings, air strikes, and other attacks, as well as the mental and emotional damage resulting from living in such violent war zones, which affect civilians more than trained and armored soldiers, who are only stationed in conflict zones temporarily. Since the average life expectancy for Afghans is less than 45 years, much of the population has known nothing but war for their entire lives, a state of permanent traumatic stress that is impossible to quantify and whose consequences are unknown. Any estimate of Afghan civilian casualties should also include the hidden human costs to those who can't grow or get enough food because of the war and who are unable to reach the few medical facilities which are equipped to help with emergencies.

The number of injured Western soldiers is tracked carefully, however. Brookings' Afghanistan Index counts a total of 3,896 injured US troops from 2001 through September 8, 2009. What is particularly shocking is the sudden and dramatic escalation beginning in June 2009, just as President Obama's increased troop deployments were arriving in Afghanistan. Of all the US troops injured in Afghanistan since 2001, almost 30 percent were injured in just the two months of July and August 2009.[23]

Multiple deployments also take a huge toll on the physical and mental health of the troops, leading to rising levels of mental health trauma and heightened risk of suicide. In November 2009 Secretary of Veterans Affairs Erik Shinseki acknowledged that "more veterans have committed suicide since 2001 than we have lost on the battlefields of Iraq and Afghanistan."[24]

Some of the increased rates of injury are certainly the result of IEDs (improvised explosive devices), often in the form of bombs hidden in Afghanistan's roads. By 2009 military medics were identifying traumatic brain injury as the signature injury of the war in Afghanistan, and the military estimated that up to 20 percent of all troops who served in Afghanistan and Iraq would be victims of it. According to the Army Surgeon General's office, in 2008 the army alone spent $242 million to treat troops with brain injuries[25]—a figure that didn't take into account the marines or other services.

The costs of treating injured soldiers is only one component—albeit a large one—of the skyrocketing costs of the US war in Afghanistan. The annual cost just for US combat activities in Afghanistan rose from about $10 billion a year when the war began in 2001 to $60 billion, or $5 billion a month, in 2009. By September 2009, the total cost of the war in Afghanistan had reached $228 billion.[26] And thousands more US troops ordered to Afghanistan had not even arrived yet.

Although top Obama administration officials, civilian and military, repeatedly asserted that there would be an 80/20 split in funding for the war in Afghanistan—80 percent for development, diplomacy, humanitarian assistance, etc., and only 20 percent for the military—the reality is far different. The vast majority of funding goes straight to the Department of Defense for military costs. The Congressional Research Service, as of May 2009, examined the funding for the wars in Afghanistan and Iraq and determined that "about 94% of the funds are for DOD, 6% for foreign aid programs and embassy operations, and less than 1% for medical care for veterans."[27]

As the National Priorities Project documents, the amount of money spent on the war in Afghanistan, even before the 2009 supplemental billions, could have paid instead for more than 23 million places in Head Start for poor children for one year, or provided healthcare for more than 50 million people for a year, or outfitted almost 178 million US homes with renewable electricity for a year.[28]

For Afghans, the cost has been much higher. Despite billions of dollars spent on US-based corporate contractors, the promised networks of schools, clinics, water treatment plants, electrical grids, and new clean water systems never adequately arrived. While there has been progress in some areas of development, Afghanistan in 2009 remains impoverished, insecure, and war riven. Afghans remain overwhelmingly poor subsistence farmers, with limited access to sufficient healthcare or education, an average life expectancy of only 44 years. According to the most recent UNICEF report, the infant mortality rate is more than 257 per 1,000 live births—the highest in the world.

—PART II—

The US Invasion of Afghanistan

What reasons did the Bush administration give for invading and occupying Afghanistan?

The Bush administration's official rationale for attacking Afghanistan seemed simple, almost intuitive. The attacks of September 11, 2001 were, it was claimed, an act of war, carried out, we were told within hours of the attacks, by Islamist militants of al-Qaeda who were led by Osama bin Laden and based in Afghanistan under the protection of the Taliban government. Going to war against Afghanistan and overthrowing the Taliban all seemed to make sense.

Indeed, the attacks of September 11 terrified the US population. People would likely have followed their leaders any direction—including toward a visionary approach that might have crafted a new, non-military response to that moment of horror. But this was not Bush's intention: his goals were an easy war in Afghanistan, a military victory over "them," and a rapid expansion of the war to a global crusade in Iraq and beyond.

To win public support for this "global war on terror," the Bush administration relied as much on the language of vengeance as of self-defense. Just three days after September 11, the memorial service at the National Cathedral began with what was surely appropriate at such a moment: a wide range of clergy speaking of honoring the victims and the rescuers, of mourning and remembrance, of coming together and keeping faith in people. But when President Bush took the pulpit he diverted the audience—and the nation—from honor and unity to issue a chilling call for armed vengeance against "them." He was followed by a US military chorus singing the full version of "Battle Hymn of the Republic," including the generally ignored verses urging revenge and war. Writing in the *Atlantic* a few days later, Sage Stossel described how, "For many, the singing of this hymn, which enjoins the American 'hero' to 'crush the serpent with his heel,' and to 'die to make men free' signals America's willingness to retaliate against the recent terrorist assault."[29]

On September 20, Bush addressed a joint session of Congress. His message to the US military was short and clear: "Be ready. I've called the armed forces to alert and there is a reason. The hour is coming when America will act and you will make us proud." It was impossible to deploy the military against the actual perpetrators of the 9/11 attacks, who of course were already dead, and it was not yet clear what country or countries would be considered targets by virtue of proximity to the perpetrators' alleged supporters. But already Bush's war cry—"be ready"—began to resonate as the centerpiece of American response.

The stated goal was to wipe out the al-Qaeda network led by Osama bin Laden and to destroy the Taliban government in Afghanistan that had given al-Qaeda refuge. From the beginning the war was explicitly described in the apocalyptic, global terms that would come to characterize Bush's war against terrorism. "Our war on terror begins with al-Qaeda," Bush announced, "but it does not end there. It will not end until every terrorist group of global reach has been found, stopped and defeated." With the expansion of the war beyond al-Qaeda to all global terrorists, and the no-holds-barred language of "either you are with us or you are with the terrorists,"[30] the president set the stage for what would later come to be called the Bush Doctrine.

The initial call to war began long before any actual evidence against al-Qaeda was brought forward. When evidence was finally made public, it came not from US officials, but from a British white paper excerpted in the US press. The early justifications for the war were based not on evidence but on the supposed evil of "them":

> They hate what they see right here in this chamber: a democratically elected government. Their leaders are self-appointed. They hate our freedoms: our freedom of religion, our freedom of speech, our freedom to vote and assemble and disagree with each other.[31]

But Bush was wrong. "They"—who were understood to include Arabs, Muslims, and many others around the world, not only al-Qaeda—

didn't hate "our" freedom; they hated our role in denying them their own. Nowhere did we hear any acknowledgment from President Bush that it was US military, economic, and political support that empowered and enabled the non-democratic, non-elected, self-appointed governments in the countries where "they" lived, that it was US backing that ensured that "our" freedoms of speech, religion, assembly, and more would never be extended to "them." It was in that same context that President Bush, with high-visibility backing from his wife Laura, claimed that the war in Afghanistan aimed to "liberate" Afghan women—again with no acknowledgement of the responsibility the US still bore for arming and empowering virtually all of the extremist factions that maintained such oppressive practices (and certainly with no recognition that deploying additional troops throughout the country was doing little or nothing to improve the horrors of many women's lives, particularly women in rural areas).

Bush noted that Americans were asking, how will we fight and win this war? His answer was limited to his swaggering promise to use every weapon in the US arsenal, with no explanation of strategy, only the warning of what the coming war would *not* be. It would not look like Desert Storm, the Iraq war of 1990–1991, with a quick victory and liberated ground to crow over. It would not be like Kosovo in 1999, in which there wasn't a single

American casualty. It would not be (in an unspoken dig at President Bill Clinton) a war of quick retaliation and isolated air strikes.

So what *would* the coming war look like? President Bush said only that it would be

> a lengthy campaign unlike any other we have ever seen. It may include dramatic strikes visible on TV and covert operations, secret even in success. ... And we will pursue nations that provide aid or safe haven to terrorism.... From this day forward, any nation that continues to harbor or support terrorism will be regarded by the United States as a hostile regime.

All of which seemed designed to prepare the US public for the idea that they would be excluded from the war, that the White House had no intention of keeping the people informed about how the Pentagon would fight and win it. There was no explanation of what "winning" would actually look like. Any commitment to actually finding and bringing to trial—somewhere, anywhere—those individuals who had some real responsibility for the events of September 11 was incidental to the intention of declaring war on the entire country where they once had taken refuge.

The possibility of real international cooperation was ignored; international law enforcement personnel were mentioned, but only in passing and only based on their willingness to endorse a US plan, a US strategy. Instead, F-16 fighter jets and B-52 bombers would be deployed as bounty hunters in this new Wild West frontier territory.

By mid-2009, just months after the Bush administration left office, the US had spent over $224 billion on military actions in Afghanistan.[32] It had spent only $38 billion in total reconstruction efforts there—more than half of which was for training and arming the Afghan military and police.[33] And the fighting was escalating.

What reasons has the Obama administration given for continuing the war?

Senator Barack Obama's meteoric rise in the Democratic Party primaries of 2007–2008 was shaped largely by his emergence as the clearest opponent of the Iraq war among those candidates deemed electable. (Congressman Dennis Kucinich had a much stronger antiwar position, but his candidacy was marginalized by Democratic Party leadership.) When the field narrowed to Obama and Senator Clinton, the Iraq war quickly became the main issue distinguishing them. Obama said the Iraq war should never have been launched, and promised to bring US troops out of Iraq in sixteen months. He said the US must not only end the war, but "end the mindset that leads to war"—a formulation widely interpreted as a full rejection of the Bush administration's "global war on terrorism."

Many people believed that Obama's support for the war in Afghanistan was electorally driven, that he and his advisors believed that while his antiwar stance made him hugely popular, he still had to assert his military credentials. What better way to do that then to shift the strategic emphasis, calling for a pullout from Iraq while reiterating plans to escalate the "good war" in Afghanistan.

Like most campaign pledges, President Obama's promises about Iraq remain unfulfilled. Despite the partial pullback of combat troops from major Iraqi cities after June 30, 2009, the US occupation continues as of October 2009 with more than 124,000 US troops. Withdrawal has been more an idea than a reality, although Obama maintained a commitment to most of the letter, if not the spirit, of the 2008 US–Iraqi withdrawal agreement.

But Obama's campaign position had always been clear that the war in Afghanistan was different from the war in Iraq. Indeed, he claimed that it was the diversion of military resources to the "bad war" in Iraq that had set the stage for failure in Afghanistan, and he was going to reverse that. Candidate Obama promised to escalate the "good war" in Afghanistan—and President Obama did just that.

Throughout his campaign and in the first months of his presidency, Obama called for more troops, better equipment, new strategies, and more attention to be paid to the war in Afghanistan. He said that, "[the war in] Afghanistan demonstrates America's goals," and that unlike its invasion of Iraq, the US invaded Afghanistan "because of necessity."[34] With a planned escalation to 68,000 US troops almost complete by late summer 2009, Obama's military commanders announced the situation in Afghanistan was serious and deteriorating, and that they needed even more troops.[35] They didn't mention the skyrocketing numbers of private military contractors, or mercenaries, who by December 2009 numbered 104,000, compared to the 68,000 US troops in Afghanistan at the time.[36] By December 2009 Obama ordered 30,000 additional troops on a fast-track escalational to Afghanistan.[37]

Obama did reduce the more grandiose goals that the Bush administration had claimed for Afghanistan—goals of democracy, modernization, women's liberation, development, and more. He said, "Our number one goal has to be to make sure that [Afghanistan] cannot be used as a base to launch attacks against the United States." Later he claimed that the main goal of the US military was to protect Afghan civilians. But then President-elect Obama was clear that protecting civilians still meant "we've got to get bin Laden and we've got to get al-Qaeda."[38]

When Obama announced his administration's new strategy for the war just two months after his inauguration, he acknowledged that "Many people in the United States—and many in partner countries that have sacrificed so much—have a simple question: What is our purpose in Afghanistan? After so many years, they ask, why do our men and women still fight and die there?" His answer, he said, was simple: there are "violent extremists in Afghanistan and now Pakistan determined to kill as many Americans as they possibly can." It was all about us.

Obama described how al-Qaeda could again plot against the US, and how a return of the Taliban to power in Afghanistan, or their presence in Pakistan, could result in new attacks against Americans. And, he said, "this is not simply an American problem—far from it. It is, instead, an international security challenge of the highest order."[39] He didn't repeat what a senior US military commander had told the *Washington Post* regarding Afghanistan during the last week of the Bush administration: "We have no strategic plan. We never had one."[40]

Obama quickly announced his intention to send an additional 17,000 new US troops to Afghanistan, later raising that to 21,000. The new troops, he admitted, would not make much difference in the war, but could "help buy enough time for the new administration to reappraise the entire Afghanistan war effort and develop a comprehensive new strategy."[41] In other words, even before taking office, President Obama had announced his intention to send the troops first and figure out what to do with them later.

So the new president urged Americans to support what the *Washington Post* and so many others quickly came to call "Obama's war" in Afghanistan, and demanded that NATO and other allies support the war as well. But at the same time, Obama and his key advisors continued to send the contradictory message that "military power alone is not going to solve the problems."[42] Senator John Kerry, head of the powerful Foreign Relations Committee, said that to "just put troops, plunk them down, another 20, 30,000 in Afghanistan" would mean "we're on the wrong track."[43] Retired Marine General James L. Jones, Obama's national security advisor and former NATO commander in Afghanistan, headed a major NATO study that concluded "the international community is not winning in Afghanistan."[44]

In his speech to the Muslim world in Cairo in June 2009, Obama again recognized that "military power alone is not going to solve the problems in Afghanistan and Pakistan." He described a plan to "invest $1.5 billion a year in Pakistan for schools and hospitals and refugee assistance," and noted that the US is "providing more than $2.8 billion to help Afghans develop their economy."[45] But those sums represented only a tiny pittance of war-funding expenditures—when it came to military costs, Congress allocated $77 billion just to pay for three months of war, from July to September 2009.

President Obama also stated in Cairo, "we do not want to keep our troops in Afghanistan" and "we seek no military bases there." But just one week before Obama had been sworn in, the head of the US Army Corps of Engineers in Afghanistan had told the *Washington Post* that "the Army is building $1.1 billion worth of military bases and other facilities in Afghanistan and is planning to start an additional $1.3 billion in projects" in 2009. The *Post* acknowledged that the "massive construction of barracks, training areas, headquarters, warehouses and airfields for use by US and Afghan security forces—which could reach $4 billion—signals a long-term US military commitment."[46] President Obama did not, in his Cairo speech or elsewhere, indicate any intention to reverse that military construction.

As the US war in Afghanistan ground on, US military and political officials began to change their description of what the war was about, what "victory" might look like, and who was the enemy. In August 2009, a National Public Radio interviewer asked the US and NATO commander in Afghanistan, General Stanley McChrystal, about Afghan military leaders' attempts to negotiate or engage with the Taliban—who, along with al-

Qaeda, were ostensibly Washington's main enemy in Afghanistan. McChrystal was clear on the difference between the two organizations: "the Taliban are Afghans," he said. "They are local, and most of them are paid for their work." They're not necessarily ideologically committed to the Taliban, he added, and most of them would likely be "open to a chance for a different and a better future."[47] That position would fit well with McChrystal's new Afghanistan strategy, which claimed to put the protection of civilians, not killing "bad guys," at the top of the US agenda. But on the same day, McChrystal was interviewed by the *Wall Street Journal*, and for that venue's audience he described the same Taliban as "a very aggressive enemy right now. We've got to stop their momentum, stop their initiative."[48] To achieve that, he said, he needed more US and NATO troops. Obama's lack of strategic clarity may have been best voiced by his special envoy to the region, Richard Holbrooke, who in August 2009 used the famous Supreme Court definition of pornography to define success in Afghanistan: "We'll know it when we see it," he said.[49]

President Obama, ignoring the then 54 percent US public opposition to the war in Afghanistan, used an August 2009 speech in Arizona before thousands of members of the largely pro-war Veterans of Foreign Wars to repeat his claim that the war in Afghanistan was a "war of necessity." Ignoring the breadth of expert opinion that indicates that al-Qaeda is qualitatively weakened and its remnants are in Pakistan, not Afghanistan, the president persisted in defending the war as necessary because "those who attacked America on 9/11 are plotting to do so again. If left unchecked, the Taliban insurgency will mean an even larger safe haven from which al Qaeda would plot to kill more Americans. So this is not only a war worth fighting. This is fundamental to the defense of our people."[50] He did not officially acknowledge channeling Lyndon Johnson, whose anti-poverty Great Society efforts were destroyed by the war in Vietnam, nor did the word "quagmire" appear in his speech.

Are there other reasons for the war?

The public reasons asserted for launching the war in Afghanistan in the aftermath of September 11 had to do with self-defense, vengeance, stopping terrorism, and "getting 'them' before 'they' get us." But there were underlying reasons that received less attention but were certainly as important, or perhaps more so, as the official rationales.

One was the effort to impose US-determined discipline on the world, an ideology that came to be known as the Bush Doctrine—expressed in the president's Wild West–style threat that "you're either with us, or with the terrorists." Governments around the world scrambled to remake their image in American eyes. Repressive regimes, once distastefully held at arm's length by a virtuous State Department, morphed into allies appropriately clamping down on opposition movements that were suddenly discovered to be terrorists linked to al-Qaeda.

Another of Bush's reasons for the war in Afghanistan could perhaps best be summed up as "because he could get away with it." *New York Times* veteran hawk and wordsmith William Safire described this by citing a passage of dialogue in a Sherlock Holmes story: "'Is there any point,' asked the Inspector, 'to which you would like to draw my attention?' 'To the curious incident of the dog in the nighttime.' 'The dog did nothing in the nighttime.' 'That was the curious incident,' remarked Sherlock Holmes." For Safire, the fact that diplomatic dogs were not barking all over the world was evidence of international acquiescence to Bush's unilateralism. Safire viewed this positively, noting, "This welcome silence is a form of grudging assent, and is the first major achievement of George W. Bush's first year as president."[51]

Unilateralism was a central tenet of George W. Bush's presidency. Although they differed in their attitudes toward the UN, the foreign policy of both President Bushes relied on the creation of international coalitions in whose name the US could impose its agenda. President George H.W. Bush made the United Nations his instrument of choice, and employed a wide array of time-tested diplomatic tools including bribes, kickbacks, and punishments, to win adequate, if not unanimous, Security Council endorsement for his 1991 war against Iraq. George W. Bush's administration, however, had no intention of relying on or seeking an official (however dubiously achieved) credential from the UN to authorize its actions. The second President Bush would instead proudly claim the mantle of unilateralism, shaping a US-created coalition specifically designed to keep the United Nations out of the loop.

For President Obama, the role of electoral politics cannot be ignored: Obama built his people-driven campaign more than anything else on the basis of his opposition to Bush's war in Iraq. But he and his advisors were well aware that if he were to have a chance at victory as an antiwar candidate, he would have to prove his potential-commander-in-chief credentials somewhere else. That somewhere else would be Afghanistan. The irony, of course, was that Obama's determination to maintain and indeed escalate the US military occupation of Afghanistan did not seem to falter even with his own recognition that "I'm absolutely convinced that you cannot solve the problem of Afghanistan, the Taliban, the spread of extremism in that region, solely through military means."[52]

All of this was before the longstanding question of oil, natural gas, and other resources would emerge from the shadows. While Afghanistan has only relatively small reserves of strategic resources, it is located smack in the middle of the oil- and gas-rich Central Asia/Caspian Sea Basin region. Land-locked Afghanistan has a millennial history as part of the trade and cultural exchange of the Silk Road, and in the modern world remains a strategic transit point for its resource-rich neighbors to get oil and gas to far-off markets. The US relationship with Afghanistan both pre- and post-9/11 (see particularly page 54 on pre-9/11 history) has been grounded in the potential for these oil and natural-gas pipelines. (See page 48 for more on the role of oil and gas.)

Afghanistan's neighbors are also almost all of strategic interest to the US. US tensions with Pakistan and Iran dominate the southern east-to-west arc of Afghanistan's frontier. Dependence on airbases, access to natural gas and oil, and especially competition—resource-driven and otherwise—with an ascendant Russia (as well as occasional expressions of concern about human-rights violations) shape US relations with Uzbekistan, Tajikistan, and Turkmenistan on Afghanistan's northern borders.

What role have oil and natural gas played in the war?

Afghanistan is not resource-rich in oil or natural gas. By contrast, much of Central Asia and the Caspian Basin, including the Caspian Sea and the countries surrounding it—Azerbaijan, Iran, Turkmenistan, Kazakhstan, Turkey, and Georgia—are sitting on enormous oil and natural-gas reserves, which have only recently been tapped. On the day before the September 11 attacks, the *Oil & Gas Journal* reported that Central Asia had 20 billion barrels of undeveloped oil reserves, and 6.6 trillion cubic meters of natural gas. [53]

The problem these countries faced was not lack of resources, but rather challenges stemming from poverty and location. Newly independent after the Cold War ended and the Soviet Union collapsed, they had insufficient resources to exploit their gas and oil reserves on their own. Many were landlocked and thus dependent on neighboring states for transporting their oil and gas out to the rest of the world. And because those Central Asian countries with oil had spent three-quarters of the twentieth century as part of the Soviet Union, it was not surprising that the pipelines that had been built headed north and west into Russia. Western oil companies had long coveted access to the rich potential profits of the Central Asian oil and gas fields, as well as control of the pipelines and other transit arrangements. This is where Afghanistan would fit in.

Even after the Cold War, the legacy of long-standing Russian domination of Caspian and Central Asian oil production remained a major stumbling block to Western oil company plans. Before September 11, the US Energy Advisory Board website listed the US policy goals for Caspian and Central Asia's energy resources:

> fostering the independence of the Caspian and Central Asian states and their ties to the west;
> breaking Russia's monopoly over oil and gas transport routes;
> promoting western energy security through diversified suppliers;
> encouraging the construction of east-west pipelines that do not transit Iran;
> denying Iran dangerous leverage over the Central Asian economies.[54]

In 2001, the still-untapped oil reserves in Kazakhstan, Kyrgyzstan, Tajikistan, Turkmenistan, and Uzbekistan were estimated to be worth up to $2 trillion. Six of the biggest US oil companies—Unocal, Total, Chevron, Pennzoil, Amoco, and Exxon—had all plowed money into exploiting oil fields throughout Central Asia.[55] But they still faced the problem of getting the oil out of Central Asia and on to the more lucrative markets—to the east in China, Korea, and Japan, to the west in Europe, and on to the US as well, without empowering Russia or China through control of pipelines.

Afghanistan was perfectly situated geographically as a crucial transit point for Central Asian gas and oil. A US government Energy Information Fact Sheet published in September 2000 was quite explicit:

> Afghanistan's significance from an energy standpoint stems from its geographic position as a potential transit route for oil and natural gas exports from Central Asia to the Arabian Sea. This potential includes proposed multi-billion dollar oil and gas export pipelines through Afghanistan.[56]

Just four years earlier, when the Taliban had first taken over Kabul in 1996, then Unocal executive (later US ambassador to Afghanistan and then to the United Nations) Zalmay Khalilzad had dined with Taliban leaders in Texas to discuss exactly those pipelines. (See page 62.) As Vice President Dick Cheney recognized in 1998 (during his private sector years in between his stints as US secretary of defense and vice president), "the good Lord didn't see fit to put oil and gas only where there are democratic regimes friendly to the United States."[57] So Washington's first approach to the Taliban in power was an oil-driven "we can do business with these guys."

Afghanistan under the Taliban was certainly not a "democratic regime." Nor were the governments of its Central Asian neighbors. But identifying governments in the region who would be "friendly to the United States," however undemocratic, was pretty easy. During Dick Cheney's five years as CEO of the Halliburton Oil Services company, he also served, along with executives from Chevron and Texaco, on the advisory board of Kazakhstan's state oil company. His later colleague in the Bush administration, Undersecretary of Commerce for Economic Affairs Kathleen Cooper, was a former chief economist for Exxon-Mobil. Together, Chevron-Texaco and Exxon-Mobil were among the biggest investors in Kazakhstan's famed Tengiz oil field.[58] Throughout the 1990s, the collaboration helped the two sets of American oil partnerships accomplish a stated US goal of challenging traditional Russian domination in Kazakhstan. The two giant oil companies joined a complicated partnership giving them major interests, along with Russia, Kazakhstan, and Oman, in building a pipeline from the Tengiz field in Kazakhstan to Russia's Black Sea port of Novorossiysk. This all took place during the ten-year tenure of future Bush administration Secretary of State Condoleezza Rice on the board of directors of Chevron. Later Chevron-Texaco thanked Rice for her advice in that period by naming an oil tanker after her.[59]

Access to Afghanistan for new pipelines remained elusive, but the economic potential for

US oil interests in this region continued. In 1998 the *Amarillo Globe-News* reported that Cheney told oil executives that "the current hot spots for major oil companies are the oil reserves in the Caspian Sea region."[60] It was not surprising then that, once in power in Washington in 2001, the oilmen and oilwomen of the Bush administration would continue their efforts to ensure US access to current and future Central Asian oil and gas and related pipelines. That goal didn't disappear after September 11, even as the Bush administration prepared to wage war across the country they had once viewed as a giant future oil transit hub.

—PART III—

The US and Other Players in Afghanistan

What is the history of US involvement in Afghanistan before 9/11?

Throughout the sequence of empires that have risen and fallen in the region, the land that is now Afghanistan, a nation-state since the middle of the eighteenth century, has always been prized for its strategic location. In modern history Britain played the key imperial role. In 1893, after years of failed British efforts to win control of Afghanistan, the foreign minister in the colonial government in India, Sir Mortimer Durand, negotiated with the amir of Afghanistan to set the border dividing Afghanistan and what was then British India (today the northwest areas of Pakistan). The Durand Line split the Pashtun territory that still straddles the Afghanistan–Pakistan border, with large Pashtun populations on both sides.

The US was not directly involved in Afghanistan until the Cold War. In 1973 Afghanistan's monarchy was overthrown, and a republic declared. A left-wing rebellion in 1978 resulted in the creation of the Democratic Republic of Afghanistan, led by the People's Democratic Party of Afghanistan (PDPA). The PDPA was a communist party whose program tended toward liberal, secular, and socialist reforms, building on some of the social reforms (including outlawing the purdah, a form of isolating women from social contact) that had started in Afghanistan in the 1950s. Although much of the reformist social agenda did not reach beyond Kabul, land reform and support for farmers in the rural areas were high on the PDPA agenda. At least in the cities, Afghan women played a major role in the emerging political and economic life of the country. Kabul quickly developed ties with the Soviet Union, and so, for the US, Afghanistan was now a Cold War target.

President Jimmy Carter's national security advisor, Zbigniew Brzezinski, began a secret campaign of arming, training, and funding Islamist guerrillas known as the Mujahideen against the government in Afghanistan, funneling arms and US and Saudi money through Pakistan's intelligence agency, the ISI. One of the Mujahideen leaders was the young Osama bin Laden, whose organization trained and funded the ISI- and US-backed Mujahideen (see page 66).

For Washington, consolidating a relationship with Pakistan during the Cold War was important because of Pakistan's hostility to India, which maintained longstanding ties to the Soviet Union. Even more important, undermining the Afghan government would weaken Soviet influence in the region.

In response to growing instability in Afghanistan, on Christmas Eve 1979, the Soviet Union sent in troops, who entered Kabul the following day. Soviet troops would remain in

Afghanistan for the next ten years. Defenders of US support for the anti-government and anti-Soviet Mujahideen claimed the US was only helping Afghanistan fight against Soviet occupation. But in 1998 Brzezinski admitted:

> According to the official version of history, CIA aid to the mujahideen began in 1980, that is to say, after the Soviet Union invaded Afghanistan, 24 December 1979. But the reality, secretly guarded until now, is completely otherwise. Indeed, it was July 3, 1979, that President Carter signed the first directive for secret aid to the opponents of the pro-Soviet regime in Kabul. And that very day, I wrote a note to the president in which I explained to him that in my opinion, this aid was going to induce a Soviet military intervention.... We didn't push the Russians to intervene, but we knowingly increased the probability that they would.[61]

The presence of the Soviet troops gave rise to what the journalist Steve Coll described as "fluid networks of stateless Islamic radicals whose global revival after 1979 eventually birthed bin Laden's al Qaeda."[62] In 1998 Brzezinski dismissed the consequences of the US backing Islamist extremists: "What is most important to the history of the world?" he asked. "The Taliban or the collapse of the Soviet empire? Some stirred-up Moslems or the liberation of Central Europe and the end of the cold war?"[63]

Afghanistan became the centerpiece of Ronald Reagan's doctrine of active military backing for anti-Soviet resistance groups. Throughout his eight years in office Reagan escalated support for the Mujahideen, thereby consolidating relations with Pakistan and Saudi Arabia as bulwarks against pro-Soviet India. In 1985 Reagan's CIA director, William Casey, crafted National Security Decision Directive 166, which provided the legal justification for a huge escalation of the CIA's role inside Afghanistan.[64] During that time the Reagan administration also became special patrons of Gulbuddin Hekmatyar, head of one of the most powerful and most extreme Islamist guerrilla organizations. Hekmatyar had the closest ties to the ISI, received most of the funds from the US and the Saudis, and was the main recipient of the much-coveted Stinger anti-aircraft missiles provided by the US.[65] He was one of the Mujahideen leaders brought to a highly publicized White House visit in 1985, where President Reagan welcomed the Islamist guerrillas as the "moral equivalent of America's founding fathers."[66]

From 1985 on, the US- and Pakistan-backed Islamist guerrillas escalated the fight against the Soviet forces in Afghanistan. The violence forced almost half the population of the country from their homes, and millions fled Afghanistan to seek refuge in neighboring Iran or especially Pakistan, where the United Nations scrambled to put together survival camps for the flood of refugees.

When the Soviet troops were forced out of Afghanistan in 1988–1989, the civil war escalated, as the Mujahideen organizations continued to challenge the government in Kabul. In 1991 the US and the Soviet Union agreed to end military aid to both sides, and within a year the Mujahideen organizations overthrew the government. The Democratic Republic of Afghanistan was over. Its president, Najibullah, was arrested and publicly tortured to death. The still well-armed Mujahideen turned on each other, and fighting among them, ethnically based and otherwise, continued. Where the Islamist factions consolidated power, they imposed repressive social laws, based on extremist interpretations of Islamic law, or sharia. Women paid the heaviest price under the harsh laws, which overturned the fragile gains women (at least urban women) had made since 1978, and aimed instead to exclude them from most social, national, political, and economic life, and bring them under the full control of their fathers and husbands.

In 1993 the warring factions agreed on a government, with Burhanuddin Rabbani, a Tajik leader, proclaimed president, and Hekmatyar, a Pashtun, named prime minister. But the quarreling coalition of Islamists continued fighting. Civilian casualties continued to mount. Within a year a new

Pashtun-dominated group within the array of jockeying factions took the lead in challenging Rabbani's government. It was called the Taliban.

What is the history of US–Taliban relations?

The Taliban (or "students") organization was made up primarily of young Pashtun men whose parents had fled Afghanistan during the anti-Soviet and civil wars, and who had mostly grown up in the crowded, squalid refugee camps in Pakistan. They grew up impoverished, disempowered, angry, without jobs, without hope. Most of their education, if indeed they had access to education at all, was provided by Saudi-funded and Pakistani-run madrasas, or Islamic schools, many of which taught a severe, extremist interpretation of the Qur'an and Islamic law.

In 1996 the Taliban captured control of Kabul. Rabbani's government collapsed. Some government officials fled Afghanistan, seeking refuge in countries that had long supported them from outside, including Pakistan. Others, including Rabbani himself, remained in the country, but headed north to join the shaky coalition of anti-Taliban Islamist guerrillas known as the Northern Alliance. As the Pakistan-backed Taliban had gained power, Pakistan's competitor India had emerged as a key supporter of the Northern Alliance. So with the Cold War over, the US turning its attention elsewhere, and the Soviet Union about to collapse, the Afghan civil war players took on regional sponsors to replace their global backers. Pakistan escalated its support for the newly empowered Taliban, while Indian interests (and soon the CIA) became inextricably linked to the Northern Alliance.

As the Taliban consolidated its control over Kabul and the countryside, it quickly introduced even more extreme versions of sharia, in which many women were virtually imprisoned in their homes. Harsh punishments, including stoning to death and amputations, escalated. But the Taliban also knew how to win the loyalty of the local population, war-weary and exhausted from the years of fighting. The Taliban had promised to put an end to the fighting among the militias that had led to so much death and destruction for Afghan civilians. As a result, in many parts of the country, the Taliban was welcomed, and won some level of popular support with the expectation that its ascension to power would lead to some break in the fighting, some hope for stability. The Taliban were not corrupt, in stark contrast to many of the Western-armed tribal and ethnic bosses they fought against. (In fact, Taliban leader Mullah Omar famously lived in a primitive hut, eschewing the luxuries of other powerful leaders.) So people did not have to pay bribes to deal with local officials, and the Taliban's campaigns to end petty crime and corruption brought them more support.

Internationally, the Taliban government in Kabul was recognized only by Pakistan, Saudi Arabia, and the United Arab Emirates. Other countries continued to recognize the deposed Burhanuddin Rabbani, now one of the leaders of the Northern Alliance, as the legitimate president. The Northern Alliance, led by Rabbani and the popular Islamist leader and defense minister Ahmad Shah Massoud, continued fighting against the Taliban, and the US supported them.

In February and May 1998, two massive earthquakes killed thousands of Afghans. In August, al-Qaeda was held responsible for the bombings of US embassies in Kenya and Tanzania. Two weeks later, the US launched retaliatory missile strikes against Afghanistan, targeting what were supposed to be al-Qaeda bases there. President Clinton said, "Our mission was clear—to strike at the network of radical groups affiliated with, and funded by, Osama bin Laden, the pre-eminent organizer and financier of international terrorism in the world today."[67] But bin Laden was nowhere to be found by those strikes, although dozens of Afghans were killed and injured. By 1999 the US had pressured the United Nations to impose harsh sanctions on Afghanistan, ostensibly to force the Taliban to extradite bin Laden for trial in the US.

In the meantime the civil war continued. The Northern Alliance, still led by Ahmad Shah Masood, kept up the effort to depose the Taliban, although the competing opposition leaders had splintered into factions also at war against each other. International opposition to the Taliban rose, particularly in response to their destruction of the sixth-century Buddhist statues carved into cliff sides in Bamiyan, carried out in 1998 between the two earthquakes. The US also publicly attacked the Taliban for their oppression of women—while ignoring a very similar pattern of attacks on women by the warlords of the US-backed Northern Alliance and the rest of the Islamist guerrilla opposition.

But in fact, public expressions of outrage aside, as soon as the Taliban seized power the US was quite willing to deal with them strategically despite their brutality, attacks on women, and other human rights violations. Afghanistan was still located in a strategic neighborhood, regardless of who was in power in Kabul. Oil and gas pipelines were still on the agenda. The US-based Unocal oil company wanted to meet with the Taliban. So on October 7, 1996, just after the Taliban had seized control of Kabul, Afghan-American neoconservative and Reagan administration insider Zalmay Khalilzad, who then worked for Unocal, wrote in the *Washington Post* that it was "time for the United States to reengage" with the Taliban.[68] At the same time, as the Taliban consolidated their rule and Afghan women were being forced out of public life,

Khalilzad coordinated the visit of top Taliban officials to the United States. The *Post* found him "at a luxury Houston hotel, ... chatting pleasantly over dinner with leaders of Afghanistan's Taliban regime about their shared enthusiasm for a proposed multibillion-dollar pipeline deal."[69]

A few years later, after the US invaded Afghanistan to overthrow Khalilzad's dining companions, the respected *World Press Review* would note that the "United States was slow to condemn the Taliban in the mid-1990s because the Taliban seemed to favor US oil company Unocal to build two pipelines across Afghanistan."[70]

The internecine battles among Afghan militias continued, even with the Taliban defeated and the US-backed Afghan government of President Hamid Karzai installed in power since 2002. One of the most extremist leaders of the anti-Soviet Mujahideen guerrillas, Gulbuddin Hekmatyar—the one who had been provided with hundreds of millions of dollars from the CIA and welcomed to the White House as a "freedom fighter" by President Reagan back in the 1980s despite being known for throwing acid in the faces of unveiled women in his university days—had fought against the Taliban since they took over in 1996. But then he turned against the US-led occupation, pledging to kill American troops just as he had once killed Soviets. In 2006 he announced his allegiance to Osama bin Laden.[71]

But the Taliban's opposition to the US emerged only after the US invasion, and focused on getting the US out of Afghanistan. In fact, US officials recognize that the Taliban's danger to the US, if any, was limited to their providing refuge for al-Qaeda; on their own the Taliban was no threat to the US (except to US troops occupying their country).

Indeed, by the middle of 2007, when the Taliban resurgence in Afghanistan was well underway, many US officials still claimed they had no idea how the resurgence could have happened. The *New York Times* reported that, since the quick overthrow of the Taliban government in 2001,

> American intelligence agencies had reported that the Taliban were so decimated they no longer posed a threat, according to two senior intelligence officials who reviewed the reports. The American sense of victory had been so robust that the top C.I.A. specialists and elite Special Forces units who had helped liberate Afghanistan had long since moved on to the next war, in Iraq. When it came to reconstruction, big goals were announced, big projects identified. Yet in the year Mr. Bush promised a 'Marshall Plan' for Afghanistan, the country received less assistance per capita than did post-conflict Bosnia and Kosovo, or even desperately poor Haiti, according to a RAND Corporation study. Washington has spent an average of $3.4 billion a year reconstructing Afghanistan, less than half

of what it has spent in Iraq, according to the Congressional Research Service.[72]

One respondent summarized the view of many rural communities, "the presence of the Taliban is a blessing for the US as it is an excuse for the US to be here, otherwise other countries would all ask the US to leave the region. So the Taliban legitimizes the US presence."[73] Why should anyone have been surprised that the Taliban were resurgent, still challenging the US, years after they were driven out of Kabul in 2001?

The Taliban resurgence beginning in 2008 was linked directly to the more active combat initiated by the US and NATO forces in Afghanistan. Despite significant opposition by many in the Afghan public, the Taliban remained a viable part of the country's mélange of ethnic, tribal, and Islamist militias.

What is al-Qaeda and what does it have to do with Afghanistan?

Al-Qaeda is an Islamist organization with its origins dating back to the 1980s, when Afghan, Arab, and other Mujahideen battled Soviet troops and each other across Afghanistan. Al-Qaeda, which means "the base" in Arabic, champions an extremist version of Sunni Islam. Its goals center on over-turning the existing governments controlling Islam's holy areas, particularly that of Saudi Arabia, which al-Qaeda views as corrupt, insufficiently Islamic, and responsible for the polluting presence of non-believers (especially US troops) in the region. It was in this context that al-Qaeda came to view the US as a target—because of Washington's support for the "apostate" regimes in Saudi Arabia and other countries. Al-Qaeda also believes in the religious obligation to create a new caliphate, or Islamic theocracy, to replace governments throughout the Muslim world and beyond.

In the early and mid-1980s, al-Qaeda's founder and leader, Osama bin Laden, was one of the leaders of an earlier organization, the Maktab al-Khidamat, which had used money from sponsors in US-allied Saudi Arabia and Pakistan to provide support for the Arab and other foreign Muslims fighting against the Soviet Union in Afghanistan.[74] Around the time the Soviet troops pulled out of Afghanistan, in 1988–1989, bin Laden's group morphed into al-Qaeda. While it remains unclear whether the US had direct ties with or provided direct support to bin Laden and his organization, there is no question that Pakistan's Inter-Services Intelligence agency (ISI) was a major sponsor. Pakistan's government, including the ISI, served as the key link between the CIA and other US government agencies and the Afghanistan Mujahideen during the war against the Soviet Union in Afghanistan.

In 1991, with the anti-Soviet war over and

Afghanistan's various Mujahideen militias continuing to fight each other, bin Laden and al-Qaeda moved to the Sudan, where they would be based for five years. During that time, several military attacks against the US, including the bombing of the Pentagon's Khobar Tower barracks in Saudi Arabia, as well as several terrorist attacks and attempted attacks on civilians, most notably the 1993 bombing of New York's World Trade Center, which killed six people, were blamed on al-Qaeda. The organization itself claimed responsibility for some of the attacks.

In 1996, Osama bin Laden left Sudan and moved his operation to Afghanistan. Initially there was no official invitation, and indeed reportedly some tensions between al-Qaeda and the Taliban, which had just beaten its Northern Alliance opponents in the battle of militias that defined Afghanistan's post–Soviet civil war. But with access to bin Laden's financial and, allegedly, military support, the Taliban grew closer to al-Qaeda, and eventually Taliban leader Mullah Omar broke with his long-time Saudi backers by refusing to hand bin Laden over to Saudi Arabia.

Two weeks after the bombing of two US embassies in 1998, in Kenya and Tanzania, the US retaliated with cruise missile attacks on Sudan and Afghanistan. US officials described the targets in Afghanistan as "part of a network of terrorist compounds near the Pakistani border that housed supporters of Saudi millionaire Osama bin Laden." They told CNN they had "convincing evidence" that "bin Laden, who has been given shelter by Afghanistan's Islamic rulers, was involved in the bombings of the east African embassies."[75] Neither bin Laden nor any of his top associates were hit in the US missile strike.

Several months after the retaliatory air strikes, in November 1998, bin Laden was indicted in US courts for the African embassy bombings. The Taliban government in Afghanistan refused US demands to extradite him to stand trial in the US. In 2001, just two days before the September 11 attacks, al-Qaeda operatives assassinated the military commander of the Northern Alliance, Ahmed Shah Massoud, who was at the time Afghanistan's most powerful opponent of the Taliban.

Then came September 11 and its aftermath, including the US launch of a massive air war against Afghanistan that began October 7, 2001, followed later by the ground assault. The Taliban government in Kabul was ousted within weeks. The targets of the war were supposed to be al-Qaeda, and some of the most brutal aspects of the war occurred during US efforts to kill (or in a few cases capture) al-Qaeda leaders. But the Taliban also were identified as targets of the war. Even after the Taliban was overthrown and ousted from the capital, with the new US-backed government installed in Kabul, the

US continued its full-scale invasion and occupation of Afghanistan in the name of fighting al-Qaeda, with devastating consequences for the Afghan people. As the *New York Times* noted in a 2007 analysis of what had gone wrong with the war, after the overthrow of the Taliban, the war continued and, "in the end, the United States deployed 8,000 troops to Afghanistan in 2002, with orders to hunt Taliban and Qaeda members, and not to engage in peacekeeping or reconstruction. The 4,000-member international peacekeeping force did not venture beyond Kabul."[76]

Not surprisingly, with both the Taliban leadership and most of the al-Qaeda operatives melting away, some apparently finding refuge in the largely Pashtun areas of the rugged region straddling the Afghan–Pakistani border, it was mainly Afghan civilians who paid the price. By 2009, virtually all analysts agreed that fewer than 100 al-Qaeda operatives remained in Afghanistan—but the war continues, with Afghan civilians paying the price.

What did the Taliban have to do with the attacks of September 11, 2001?

None of the September 11 hijackers were Afghans, none of them lived in Afghanistan, none were taking orders from the Taliban. The allegation against the Taliban was limited to the fact that Osama bin Laden and the leaders of al-Qaeda, which did take responsibility for the September 11 attacks, had found sanctuary in Afghanistan in 1996 after leaving the Sudan.

On September 9, 2001, the legendary Northern Alliance guerrilla leader Ahmad Shah Masood was assassinated during the taping of a television interview. The journalists turned out to be suicide bombers using a bomb hidden in a camera. According to al-Qaeda expert Peter Bergen, "by engineering his death bin Laden gave the Taliban something they desperately wanted, and ensured that the Taliban would protect al-Qaeda in Afghanistan after 9/11."[77] So absent this action of al-Qaeda's, the Taliban might have even refused to provide sanctuary to al-Qaeda following the 9/11 attacks.

There is no evidence that the Taliban actually supported the 9/11 attacks. To the contrary, according to the official report of the National Commission on Terrorist Attacks, the 9/11 Commission, there was significant opposition among the Taliban: "As final preparations were under way during the summer of 2001, dissent emerged among al Qaeda leaders in Afghanistan over whether to proceed. *The Taliban's chief, Mullah Omar, opposed attacking the United States.* Although facing opposition from many of his senior lieutenants, bin Laden effectively overruled their objections, and the attacks went forward [emphasis added]."[78]

What has the US done to help Afghanistan's reconstruction, and what is its plan for the future?

In late 2001, after the US invasion drove the Taliban from power, talk soon turned to reconstruction. At the Bonn conference, Karzai was installed as a new head of state but there were no functioning ministries in the new government. Over 22 years of civil war had created enormous humanitarian needs as well as decimated the country's infrastructure.

At the Bonn conference, the US, the UN, and others in the international donor community pledged billions in development and reconstruction assistance. While the UN and a few humanitarian NGOs had continued to operate in Afghanistan during the Taliban regime, hundreds more NGOs now rushed in to help on the new frontier of reconstruction and nation-building (and for some, to help themselves to a piece of the growing reconstruction aid pie). International staff of aid agencies and governments brought years of experience from work in Bosnia, East Timor, and other post-conflict situations, but few had any experience or knowledge of Afghanistan.

Afghans too had great hopes. More than 6 million refugees hoped to return and rebuild their lives after years living in refugee camps in Pakistan or Iran. Tajik, Uzbek, and Shia Hezara communities who had all suffered greatly under the Taliban saw an opportunity to rebuild as well as regain a share of political power in a new government. Many of the refugees returning went to urban areas in hopes of accessing jobs and reconstruction funds. This created enormous additional pressures on Kabul and other cities. Kabul, which had roughly 1.5 million people in 2001, tripled in population in the next few years to nearly 5 million.

While everyone knew that the Taliban had not been eliminated, the US and the international aid community proceeded as if Afghanistan had become a "post-conflict" situation rather than a continuing insurgency and war. Yet the Bonn conference did not reach a peace agreement among all parties in Afghan-istan, but an agreement among victors (mainly groups within the Northern Alliance, components of the Afghan diaspora, the US and other donor countries, and a few US-chosen individuals).

With the US's decision to limit its military role to Kabul, and later to the other major cities, most reconstruction efforts concentrated their funding and projects in urban areas, where only 20 percent of Afghans lived. As resentment in rural areas grew, so did support for the Taliban and other armed opposition groups.

As the insurgency intensified, especially after 2006, the UN and many aid agencies declared many rural areas "no go zones" for aid workers, particularly internationals. When rural communities, which include some of the most desperate and impoverished parts of the Afghan population, and make up 77 percent of its people, are declared unsafe for foreign aid workers, the message these communities hear is a colonial-type assessment that says international lives are more important than the lives of local people.

Since 2001, the US has been the single largest source of funding for reconstruction—appropriating $33 billion, or 60 percent, of the total $58.3 billion in international aid.[79] Not surprisingly, US priorities and the requirements Washington places on implementing reconstruction projects have a significant impact on the overall reconstruction effort. Yet the US and others in the international community have pledged less per capita to reconstruction in Afghanistan than to any other recent conflict situation (e.g., Rwanda, the Balkans, Somalia, Sudan). By contrast, a 2009 Center for American Progress report recognized that "even the Soviet Union spent more on reconstruction" than the US government has so far.[80]

More significantly, over half of US reconstruction funds are not for development or humanitarian need at all, but for programs run by the Pentagon. More than $15 billion has gone to training, equipping, and arming the Afghan National Army and the Afghan National Police. In

March 2009 the US announced plans to increase the size of the military and police to 400,000, hoping the security agencies could substitute for a failing government.[81] So supporting Afghanistan's military capacity would have to continue to take the largest share of reconstruction funds. In August 2009 General McChrystal recommended that the total number of troops in the Afghan army alone be increased to 240,000.[82] Yet it is unclear who will continue to pay for such an enlarged military and police force in coming years. In 2009, 75 percent of the Afghan national budget depended on foreign revenue sources. By far the largest segment of Afghan government expenses already goes to the military and police.

The US Army / Marine Corps Counterinsurgency Field Manual of 2006, written by General David Petraeus, declares that the civilian side must provide 80 percent of the solution while the military should be only 20 percent. The Obama administration claims to have embraced this approach as a guideline for its strategy in Afghanistan. But in terms of actual funding and staffing, the numbers tell a different story. In March 2009, Obama announced an order to increase US troops by 21,000 and that the US would undertake a "civilian surge" which would seek to deploy an additional 450 civilian staff from USAID, the State Department, and the Department of Agriculture.

The so-called civilian surge was not a humanitarian surge but rather a small number of technical experts who would operate under the Pentagon's umbrella and seek to deepen ties of civil–military cooperation. Many of these 450 positions remain unfilled—with few civilian aid workers or experts willing to operate under military arrangements. So rather than an 80/20 civilian/military split, the US continues to devote roughly 95 percent of its funding to military expenditures with less than 5 percent for non-military reconstruction and development.

The largest portion of US reconstruction funds not channeled through the Pentagon goes through USAID for road construction. Afghanistan has almost no paved roads outside of cities and the ring road that connects Herat, Kandahar, Kabul, and Mazar-i-Sharif, which was built over 30 years ago. Three decades of civil war have destroyed many existing roads and made road repair incredibly difficult and dangerous.

US road construction has primarily military, not humanitarian goals. David Kilcullen, author of *The Accidental Guerilla* and close advisor to General Petreaus, argues that "the road construction process" more than the actual roads built, plays a key role in building popular local support for the US military.[83] Road building is expensive, which allows the US military to hand out lucrative contracts to Afghan contractors. Many contractors prefer working with the US military or USAID rather than through Afghan ministries, which require bribes up front. Yet reconstruction projects that bypass Afghan government authorities do nothing to break the cycle of corruption. On the contrary, in some cases when the Kabul government is not involved, it is the Taliban who demand payouts from road contractors to safeguard them from attacks. Thus some US road construction funding finds its way into the coffers of insurgents.

Only a small percentage of US reconstruction funds (an average of $1.5 billion a year since 2001) has gone toward any humanitarian and development needs, and much of that never actually reached the Afghan people. It is estimated that 25 to 30 percent of all reconstruction project funding goes to security for aid workers. On top of that there are the administrative costs of inter-national agencies that often serve as subcontractors, or implementers, of various US government-funded projects. Most US reconstruction funds are granted on a yearly basis, with an emphasis on speed and measurable outcomes. In 2004, an election year in both the US and Afghanistan, USAID tried to push the popular idea of granting $70 million for constructing schools and health clinics. Yet no thought was given to how the Afghan ministries of education and health would find money to pay salaries for teachers and health workers. Donor metrics that value measurable outcomes and speed seem to drive many reconstruction projects more than long-term sustainability and Afghan leadership.

—PART IV—

The Impact of the War

Has the war in Afghanistan made the US safer?

The people and government of Afghanistan never represented a threat to the US. The Taliban emerged as one group of Islamist guerrillas among many during the inter-Mujahideen or inter-Islamist war that followed the withdrawal of Soviet troops in 1989. Their government was harshly repressive, brutal for Afghanistan's women in particular. But the Taliban's goals were always focused on controlling Afghanistan—they never embarked on a global crusade or identified global enemies. They fought—and fight—the US and NATO because those soldiers are occupying their country. The 2009 memo drafted by Colonel Timothy R. Reese, one of the top US military advisors in Baghdad, and leaked to the *New York Times*, described a situation in Iraq directly parallel to that in Afghanistan: "Our combat operations are currently the victim of circular logic. We conduct operations to kill or capture violent extremists of all types to protect the Iraqi people and support the Government of Iraq. The violent extremists attack us because we are still here conducting military operations."[84] Reese's memo was titled, "It's Time for the US to Declare Victory and Go Home."

From about 2005 on, there has been widespread agreement in intelligence circles that most of al-Qaeda's leadership is in Pakistan, not Afghanistan. The expansion of the Afghanistan war to Pakistan—based on a so-called Af-Pak strategy that relies heavily on missile attacks by unmanned drone aircraft—has led to increasing civilian casualties and a huge escalation in anti-US sentiment across both countries. None of this has made the US or the American people any safer. Instead, along with winning new recruits for resistance forces in the region, the rising casualties and anti-US anger mean more people elsewhere in the world who might come to see attacks on US targets—military or otherwise—as potentially legitimate.

Paul Pillar was deputy chief of the CIA's counterterrorism center from 1997 to 1999. Writing in the *Washington Post* in September 2009 he challenged the common assumption that the Taliban must be destroyed because they might provide safe haven to al-Qaeda. "How important to terrorist groups is any physical haven?" he asked. "More to the point, how much does a haven affect the danger of terrorist attacks against US interests, especially the US homeland? The answer to the second question is: not nearly as much as unstated assumptions underlying the current debate seem to suppose." Reminding the world of the limited value of terrorist training camps and permanent bases, Pillar wrote,

> When a group has a haven, it will use it for such purposes as basic training of recruits. But the operations most important to future terrorist

attacks do not need such a home, and few recruits are required for even very deadly terrorism. Consider: The preparations most important to the Sept. 11, 2001 attacks took place not in training camps in Afghanistan but, rather, in apartments in Germany, hotel rooms in Spain and flight schools in the United States.[85]

Ultimately, even those who still insist the Taliban must be eliminated have to recognize that sending huge US and NATO deployments to attempt to seek out and destroy the Taliban in Afghanistan is simply not going to work. To the contrary, as Gilles Dorronsoro, top analyst for the Carnegie Endowment for International Peace, has described, "the presence of foreign troops is the most important element driving the resurgence of the Taliban."[86]

Who is the US fighting in Afghanistan?

Since the US invaded Afghanistan in October 2001, it has framed its military action as part of a global war on terror. The Bush administration described the war as against terrorists—al-Qaeda and those responsible for the attacks of 9/11—as well as the Taliban government in Afghanistan that had offered a safe haven for Osama bin Laden and al-Qaeda.

Both the Bush and Obama administrations have repeatedly portrayed the war in Afghanistan as a counterterrorism war against groups who want to harm the US. In a *Wall Street Journal* op-ed, Senators Graham, Lieberman, and McCain described Afghanistan as "the central front in the global war on terror" and later declared, "we have reached a seminal moment in our struggle against violent Islamist extremism."[87] Obama later shifted to describing the war as one of counterinsurgency rather than counterterrorism. Implicit in all these arguments is that the US is fighting "bad guys" who target innocent civilians.

Obama has also stated that a key goal in Afghanistan is to deny safe haven to terrorist groups that threaten the US, even though al-Qaeda now operates primarily out of Pakistan.

Armed opposition groups in many parts of Afghanistan describe themselves as "Taliban." The term has come to mean anyone who fights against the governments of Afghanistan or Pakistan as well as against US and International Security Assistance Force (ISAF) troops occupying Afghanistan, often with no connection between such local groups and the Taliban regime that ruled from 1996 to 2001. Similarly, many will use the term al-Qaeda to refer to any foreign fighters (e.g., Arab, Chechen, Uzbek, etc.), and not simply to the organization founded by Osama bin Laden.

By 2009, the insurgency in Afghanistan was comprised of seven major armed groups, the largest being the Islamic Movement of the Taliban (see page 59). The US claims to distinguish between hard-core, ideological Taliban and "moderate" Taliban, who may only have joined for economic or local reasons. From January to August 2009, estimates show that in 80 percent of the country the Taliban maintained a "permanent presence" (defined as at least one attack per week) while another 17 percent of Afghanistan faced "substantial Taliban/insurgent activity."[88] Given such widespread Taliban presence, combined with resentment at foreign military forces and government corruption, many men who join the Taliban do so for pragmatic or financial rather than ideological or religious reasons. Most Taliban insurgents are rural subsistence farmers who may join in a particular armed attack and then go back to farming. While the US military tries to distinguish between militants and civilians killed in any operation, Afghan communities rarely make the same distinction.

Rural communities with high rates of insurgent activities instead distinguish between "good Taliban" and "bad Taliban." In a recent study of insurgent views, good Taliban were those who: 1) exhibited genuine religious piety and could be trusted; 2) only attacked foreign forces, not Afghans; 3) delivered justice quickly and fairly; and 4) supported girls education.[89] By contrast, bad Taliban were characterized as "government Taliban,"

"Pakistan Taliban," or even "American Taliban" and were those seen as being linked with criminal activities and not having the well-being of the Afghan people as a central priority.

The other armed groups include the networks of the Haqqani and Mansur families, which are based largely in the southeast; the Tora Bora Front, based in Nangarhar; Hezb-i-Islami Gulbuddin (or HIG), led by Gulbuddin Hekmatyar; small Salafi groups that operate locally in the eastern provinces of Kunar and Nuristan; and a newly emerging number of local ex-Mujahideen groups who have been pushed out of power and are taking up arms in ways similar to the Taliban.

These groups at times relate and cooperate with one another and at times operate independently. They are all Afghan-led, Islamist, and focused on ending foreign military occupation in Afghanistan. While some have received funding, training, and technical support from foreign groups such as al-Qaeda, almost all are focused primarily on getting foreign troops out of Afghanistan—and they do not share any international agenda of waging war on the west.

Several of these groups were close US allies in the fight against Soviet occupation in the 1980s, and received massive funding and arms through the CIA. The Haqqani network is named after its leader, Jalaluddin Haqqani, one of the most effective and ruthless commanders in the fight against the Soviets in the 1980s. Haqqani received major support from Pakistan's Inter-Services Intelligence (ISI) as well as the CIA, and developed close ties with Osama bin Laden. The Haqqani group's continuing financial support from Pakistani intelligence and other sources allows them to operate independently in carrying out highly coordinated and visible attacks on government buildings, designed to undercut popular support for the Afghan government and foreign troops.

Another armed opposition group long supported by the CIA and Pakistan's ISI, and still active now in fighting against the US, is Hizb-i-Islami Gulbuddin (HIG). It is led by Gulbuddin Hekmatyar, who has one of the most brutal reputations for ruthless attacks—especially in his treatment of women—and who is widely discredited in many communities. Hekmatyar pursues a two-fold strategy of both military attacks and infiltration of governmental institutions. In October 2005, a number of former commanders from HIG registered as a political party and now control many Afghan government offices. Some believe that this party, Hizb-i-Islami Afghanistan, constitutes the largest faction in parliament.[90]

To understand fully who joins these groups, it is important to ask both why such groups are fighting the US and whom the US is *not* fighting.

There are many former Mujahideen commanders and local warlords from the Northern Alliance that are now in the US-backed Afghan government. They continue to assert heavy-handed control over local communities, often in brutal ways, yet the US is not fighting these armed groups. Pashtuns in these localities may see joining the Taliban as a means of resisting these local, corrupt yet US-supported authorities. In addition, the Afghan national police are seen as one of the most corrupt institutions in the country, repeatedly demanding payments from people to travel on roads or for other reasons. The US is seen by many Afghans as allying with, rather than fighting, a government that does not serve their interests. That the US turns a blind eye to this rampant corruption in the government it backs continues to serve as one of the strongest catalysts for the resurgence of popular support for the Taliban in recent years.

Indeed, an increasing number of Afghans are asking whom the US is really fighting. A number of former Mujahideen have observed that the Americans used to be very good and helped Afghans against foreign invaders during the 1980s, but now are acting like those earlier foreign invaders, the Soviets, by killing civilians and supporting corrupt government officials.

What impact does the war have on Afghan women?

The Bush administration sought legitimacy for its invasion of Afghanistan by claiming that the war would "liberate Afghan women." But this claim was false. Numerous Afghan women's groups have pointed out that repression of women in Afghanistan long predated the rise of the Taliban, and is based more on culture and tradition than on religion. And now the vast majority of Afghan women face the escalating violence of war in addition to longstanding systemic inequality and restrictions on work and education.

In the early 1990s, as Afghanistan's US-armed and warring factions consolidated power in various regions, they imposed repressive social laws, based on extremist interpretations of Islamic law, or sharia. Women paid the heaviest price under the harsh laws, which overturned the significant but fragile gains women (at least urban women) had made since 1978, and aimed instead to exclude them from most social, national, political, and economic life, and bring them under the full control of their fathers and husbands.

The US invasion and removal of the Taliban from power resulted in some formal changes in women's status in Kabul, including participation in the parliament and access to some universities. But these advances affect only a small percentage of

Afghan women; the vast majority of Afghan women do not live in the urban areas where these reforms are even nominally in place. Some space was created in which Afghan and international organizations work with women, as they did during the Soviet period. But with 80 percent of Afghans living outside urban areas, the conditions for women remain very harsh, and women pay a disproportionately high price for the escalating fighting of the current US/NATO war. They face rising casualties, the loss of already meager incomes, and the threat of losing their homes and being forced into exile or internal displacement.

Atiq Sarwari and Robert Crews have observed that "within a twenty-five year period Afghan women became the object of emancipation at the hands of four separate regimes: the communists, the *mujahidin*, the Taliban, and the American-led coalition all presented the amelioration of the plight of women as an obligation that made their rule legitimate."[91] In 2009, Afghanistan still has one of the highest infant mortality and maternal mortality rates in the world. About 25 percent of children don't reach the age of five. So far, neither thousands of foreign troops nor drones, Humvees, helicopters, and billions in US military might have done much to help women and children. When the US invaded and removed the Taliban in close alliance with the Northern Alliance, there was great relief among opponents of the Taliban and supporters of the Northern Alliance—but it turned out that arming one group of men with a terrible record on women's rights so they could overthrow another group of men with a terrible record on women's rights has done little to improve the situation for women. Afghan women remain unequal in law, in health, and in life.

One female Afghan aid worker reflected on the period of close Afghan–Soviet ties, "At least the Soviets built factories. Over a thousand women worked in the Bagrami cotton plant. And we were all poor; there was no corruption."[92] From 1979 to 1992, while US Presidents Carter, Reagan, and Bush each authorized massive shipments of covert arms to some of the most repressive, extremist Islamist groups, the UN desperately tried and too often failed to find funding for women's healthcare, education, and other humanitarian needs in war-racked Afghanistan.

After the initial bombing raids, the 2001 US military footprint was relatively light, but as the 2004 elections approached, the US escalated troop deployments into Afghanistan and pushed the Europeans to do likewise. As troops increased, insurgent groups also rearmed. More arms also meant mounting corruption within the US-backed government. The 2009 elections exposed wide-spread fraud and corruption. In an attempt to win votes in the Shiite community, about 10 percent of the population, when parliament was out of session President Karzai signed a decree enacting the Shi'a Personal Status Law. That law, showing a clear parallel with earlier Taliban-era restrictions, was widely protested by women's and human rights groups, but was enacted by the Karzai government nonetheless. The law gives legal standing to many traditional gender-based inequalities, and sharply restricts women's right to work, education, and movement, allowing women to leave their homes for "legitimate purposes only." The law would allow a husband to cut off food and housing to his wife if she refused his sexual demands, and implicitly legitimizes marriage with minors. With heavy restrictions already in place on women's employment, such a law would be economically devastating to women.[93] US support for the Karzai government even while it has adopted such repressive legislation has not helped Afghan women struggling for their rights.

Throughout the years of war, women have borne the brunt of the instability and military insecurity, leading to escalating mental health problems, including permanent traumatic stress. Afghan women have made clear their priorities are healthcare, education, opportunities for work, and an end to war. Under current Afghan law widows cannot work legally outside the home and many have been forced into begging or prostitution. Some NGOs support projects for women to work at home, such as making rugs, but these projects are too small and too few to have much impact. In part, US and NATO troop actions contribute to instability and provide grounds for Taliban recruiting: night raids, house searches, and body searches of women are seen as deeply humiliating and spark violent reprisals to protect the honor of Afghan women and families.

Local women's groups provide education for women to promote the use of birthing centers and clinics, though those resources remain in short supply. In 2003 only six percent of all births had a trained attendant present. USAID and some international and Afghan NGOs funded a training program that increased that figure to 20 percent of births in 2006.[94] Yet 80 percent of Afghan women are still without trained support during childbirth, and in 2009 Afghanistan still ranked second highest in the world in maternal mortality rates.[95]

The small successes that have occurred in women's access to healthcare reflect the Afghan reality of local and regional influence being more important than national. Each province has its own primary health organization, which links to the chronically under-funded Ministry of Health. Health providers have found that more women are coming for appointments for mental-health issues (which still involves social stigma). Because of gender segregation, these appointments provide important opportunities for women to meet and talk with other women; on women's days at clinics, twenty to thirty women from different communities wait outside, which allows them a chance to meet and share stories. Accessible health clinics then serve as a tool for women to come together to address domestic violence, trauma, depression, and other issues. Training women as community health workers does make a difference in improving both the financial survival of individual women, and the health indicators of women in the community.

That is true of training women as teachers also. Only 12 percent of Afghan women are literate, compared to 30 percent of men. Since 2002, many new schools have been built across the country and enrollment has gone up—including enrollment of girls. But Afghanistan's school enrollment rate remains among the lowest globally. Only one-third of Afghanistan's students nationally are girls.[96] With rising insecurity, girls' education is again under threat. Some shuras (local councils) specifically want girls' schools built in their rural communities so that girls will not have to travel to the next village on increasingly dangerous roads. But most US reconstruction funding goes to training men in the army and police, not for teachers and girls' schools, so many of those shuras' requests go unfulfilled.

During the current US war in Afghanistan, women leaders such as Sonali Kolhatkar and Mariam Rawi have repeatedly spoken out against escalating the war. In July 2009 they declared, "Waging war does not lead to the liberation of women anywhere. Women always dispropor-tionately suffer the effects of war, and to think that women's rights can be won with bullets and bloodshed is a position dangerous in its naiveté."[97] In 2009, after eight years of US-led military intervention and billions of dollars in military and reconstruction spending, Afghanistan still ranks second from the bottom on the UN's Gender Development Index, which measures women's relative life expectancy, literacy, access to education, and more.[98] The vast majority of Afghanistan's women remain impoverished, illiterate, and largely excluded from public and economic life. But despite these incredibly high rates of female illiteracy, infant and maternal mortality, almost all US funding continues to focus on putting more weapons in the hands of men (US, NATO, and Afghan). Shifting money away from paying for troops and arms, and instead providing women with teacher training, midwife training, and access to healthcare, would go much further toward improving the lives of Afghan women.

How was the Afghan government created and how does it govern?

Soon after the US air and then ground assault on Afghanistan began in 2001, even before the Taliban government had been routed from Kabul, the US and its allies were putting a plan in motion to create a new post-Taliban government. Despite Afghanistan's historic reliance on local, regional, and tribal leadership to govern, rather than a powerful national government in the capital, there was an unchallenged assumption that the new government to be imposed would be strong and centralized in the capital. Whether such a foreign-inspired government would work or not, let alone whether Afghans wanted it, was not to be discussed.

Although the United Nations had not endorsed the US-led attack, Washington did go to the Security Council to authorize its government-creation process. The UN chose an experienced international troubleshooter, the former Algerian foreign minister Lakhdar Brahimi to oversee the first-stage conference, designed to set the terms for a future loya jirga, or grand council of Afghan tribal leaders and other notables, that would then create a government. The conference opened on November 27, 2001, in Bonn, with 32 Afghan participants within four separate delegations brought together under the UN's auspices. Three of the four delegations represented Afghan exiles;

only the Northern Alliance delegation had a base inside the country. The exile factions included the Rome Group, loyal to Afghanistan's former King Zaher Shah; the Cyprus group, intellectuals with ties primarily to Iran; and the mainly Pashtun Pakistan-based Peshawar group. The Pakistani government also lobbied for allowing some representation for the Taliban, but the US was adamantly opposed and the Taliban was excluded.

Conference delegates agreed to form an interim administration to run the country and plan for the loya jirga to be held in the spring of 2002, which would then choose a transitional government to govern and draft a new constitution. But before the conference could choose an interim leader, the US moved to ensure its own candidate's position. In a surprise move, US officials orchestrated an appearance via satellite for Hamid Karzai to address the conference from inside Afghanistan. Karzai had longstanding ties to the US as part of the anti-Soviet guerrillas, and had served as deputy foreign minister under the Mujahideen-dominated govern-ment of President Burhanuddin Rabbani. He supported the Taliban when they took power. He then worked as an advisor to the US Unocal oil company, partnering with then Unocal consultant and later Bush administration ambassador to Afghanistan Zalmay Khalilzad in an effort to reach a Unocal–Taliban pipeline deal across Afghanistan.[99]

The delegates were divided over who should head up the interim cabinet, and US pressure ensured that Karzai emerged as the "compromise" candidate. Along with his longstanding US ties, Karzai, a Pashtun, simultaneously provided a way to ensure a visible Pashtun presence in the coalition since the Pashtun-dominated Taliban were excluded. According to Brahimi, "the Americans in general, were really then putting the pressure, calling Kofi Annan and telling us to hurry up. ... 'speed, speed, speed' from Colin Powell."[100]

Karzai was elected president of the transitional government in June 2002. In October 2004 he ran for president of the country. During that campaign, as the *Washington Post* acknowledged years later, Karzai "was clearly America's man in Afghanistan. US military helicopters shuttled him between campaign stops. At his inauguration, Vice President Richard B. Cheney was there to hail the day as a major moment 'in the history of human freedom.'"[101] It surprised no one when Karzai won. Throughout his period in office, he was popularly derided as the "mayor of Kabul," for his administration's inability to control the country outside the capital's city limits.

In January 2004 the loya jirga approved a constitution setting out a parliamentary form of government, although a prime ministerial position was scrapped in favor of president and vice presidents. Parliamentary elections were held the following year. But the Afghan government remained virtually entirely dependent on its international—particularly US—sponsors, for financial, political, and military support. In 2008 international donors pledged $15 billion in economic assistance. (The US offered only $2.8 billion for development assistance and diplomacy in Afghanistan for all of 2009; in contrast, US supplemental spending for military actions in Afghanistan was $39.4 billion just for three months—July to September—of that year.[102])

Afghanistan's parliament continues to meet, with its members including militia chiefs, religious fundamentalists, tribal leaders, and others, including many responsible for a wide range of crimes. Critical voices and reformist MPs are often silenced; some— such as Malalai Joya, a woman elected at 25 as the youngest member of the parliament and known for her criticisms of the US occupation, the government, and the warlords—have been thrown out of the parliament altogether. And despite rising Afghan anger at the role of US and NATO troops, despite the rise in civilian casualties across the country, the Afghan parliament and government have remained fundamentally incapable of calling for an end to the military occupation of their country, or asserting other political positions independent of their international backers.

By the time of the August 2009 elections, charges of corruption in the government, from the presidency on down, were endemic. Editors of the *Economist* described Karzai's government as "inept, corrupt and predatory," and went on to describe the "parts of Afghanistan where insurgents have been driven out and the writ of the government has been restored, residents have sometimes hankered for the warlords, who were less venal and less brutal than Mr. Karzai's lot."[103]

Taliban threats aimed to frighten voters away from the polls, but as one anonymous Afghan, a former aid worker in the city of Kandahar, wrote in the *New York Times* on the eve of the election, "it is almost beside the point that the Taliban have been escalating their campaign of intimidation, flooding the city with leaflets that promise to 'punish' those who go to the polls." The real problem, she or he wrote, was that "demoralization and despair have reached such a level… that most people tell me they will not participate in Thursday's presidential election. They doubt the transparency of the vote, disbelieving that President Hamid Karzai's corrupt administration will allow another candidate to win."[104] Another Afghan, Hassina Sherjan, a manufacturer and head of Aid Afghanistan for Education, writing in the same eve-of-the-election *Times* series, described the visible improvements since 2001, including new roads, new telephone, radio, and television companies, and more. "But the big question," Sherjan wrote, "is why, despite all this development, has the insurgency increased and faith in the government deteriorated? In part it stems from too much 'cosmetic development'... But the main cause is that people lost trust in the government for lack of a proper and transparent justice system. Out of desperation, many young Afghans either leave the country for Iran or Pakistan to seek employment or join the extremists."[105]

Many people held Karzai accountable for his inability to govern, and blamed him for the escalating levels of civilian casualties caused by US and NATO forces particularly throughout 2008 and 2009. The election's legitimacy remained in question. The Taliban did carry out attacks across the country to stifle voting, although retaliation against individual voters was rare. But fear certainly reduced voter participation. Just before the election, the Karzai government clamped down on the press, announcing an absolute ban on coverage of any acts of violence. While some reporters managed to get their stories out, others were arrested, beaten, and had their cameras smashed. Evidence of voter fraud was rampant. Even before the election, BBC documented piles of voter cards for sale across the country; al-Jazeera reporters demonstrated how the "indelible" ink used to identify voters to prevent multiple voting was easily washed off.

After the election, as initial counts gave Karzai a 54 percent majority, thus eliminating the need for a run-off election, charges of massive fraud emerged from Afghan, UN, European, US, and other election monitors. Afghanistan's independent Electoral Complaints Commission reported more than 2,100 allegations of fraud in voting and vote-counting procedures, and judged at least 618 of them would be, if proven, serious enough to have influenced the outcome.

In late October, election results were announced. A subsequent recount of 313 polling stations, those where 95 percent or more of the votes counted went to only one candidate (the vast majority favoring President Karzai), or where the number of ballots sent to be counted far out-numbered either registered voters or the small numbers of people known to have voted in partic-ularly insecure areas, reduced Karzai's share of the votes to less than 50 percent. Karzai resisted holding the required runoff, but finally agreed under US pressure from Senator John Kerry. But Karzai's key challenger, Abdullah Abdullah, who had faced his own allegations (albeit far smaller) of vote tampering, ultimately withdrew from the runoff, leaving Karzai to be anointed president again. The voting had not consolidated a new framework of democracy and support for the government in Afghanistan, but rather the opposite

of what its US and NATO sponsors had hoped.
President Karzai began his new term with his US-
backed government, already tarnished by
allegations of corruption, now virtually without
political legitimacy even as President Obama
weighed a new escalation that would send tens of
thousands of US troops to Afghanistan to support
that government.

What happens when the military is in charge of humanitarian and development work in Afghanistan?

There have been problems caused by blurring
humanitarian and military goals since the beginning
of the current war in Afghanistan. The country
already faced a humanitarian crisis driven by 23
years of war, abandonment by Cold War–era
sponsors who had left behind only weapons, and
five years of harsh Taliban rule and international
sanctions. Refugees were fleeing even before the
US attacks began, and hunger was endemic.
International food shipments stopped in antici-
pation of the US bombing, and aid organizations
withdrew their international staff.

Shortly after beginning the bombing attacks on
Afghanistan, the US executed a major propaganda-
driven exercise, air-dropping military-style
individual food packets over isolated parts of the
country. Experts in humanitarian crisis assistance

were unanimous that these air drops were not only expensive and logistically difficult, but did virtually nothing to address even the most immediate consequences of the near-starvation conditions prevailing throughout much of the country. The problem was exacerbated by escalating cluster-bomb air strikes, such as that in the village of Shaker Qala near Herat on October 22, 2002, which left behind not only dozens of dead and injured civilians, but hundreds of unexploded bombs waiting for a curious child's hand or a farmer's foot to detonate. (The US is one of very few countries that refused to sign the Ottawa Treaty banning anti-personnel land mines.)

The ultimate debacle caused by blurring military and humanitarian actions came with the realization that the unexploded cluster bomblets were covered in hard plastic that was the exact same bright yellow color as the air-dropped plastic-wrapped food packs. The Pentagon was embarrassed enough to direct radio broadcasts in Pashto and Dari warning people to "Please, please exercise caution when approaching unidentified yellow objects in areas that have been recently bombed."[106] On November 1, 2002, the Pentagon announced that it would change the food packets to blue. "It is unfortunate that the cluster bombs—the unexploded ones—are the same color as the food packets," said General Richard Myers, chairman of

the Joint Chiefs of Staff. He admitted the possibility
that Afghan civilians might confuse a desperately
anticipated meal with an unexploded cluster bomb.
"Unfortunately, they get used to running to yellow,"
he said. He did not, however, know how long it
would take to change the colors. "That, obviously,
will take some time, because there are many in the
pipeline." In a press conference with Secretary of
Defense Rumsfeld, General Myers also announced
that the US did not intend to suspend the use of
cluster bombs.[107]

The Pentagon's spring 2009 counterinsurgency
strategy of "clear, hold, build" requires greatly
increased reliance on reconstruction projects,
humanitarian aid agencies, and NGOs to carry out
the military agenda. That is because the aid is
provided not simply to assist desperately poor and
war-ravaged people, but to win support from the
local population against insurgent forces—as a
military goal. Already the UN, USAID, and other
large government-run aid agencies travel with
armed escorts because they are—and are seen as—
taking sides. In effect, armored cars and extensive
security measures serve to isolate those aid agencies
from the very communities they claim to seek to
serve. Only the International Committee of the
Red Cross and small independent NGOs are
willing to do humanitarian work in a completely
impartial way. As the US seeks to bring aid agencies

into the service of military ends, it endangers all aid workers, both Afghan and international.

So development and humanitarian assistance, rather than being shaped by the needs of Afghan people, has been instrumentalized by the Pentagon. As David Kilcullen, an expert on counter-insurgency war and close advisor to General Petraeus, notes, "in a counterinsurgency environment it is much less effective to apply governance and development assistance on a purely needs-based or universal basis. This soaks up resources with minimal political effect, and does little to counter the accidental guerrilla phenomenon."[108] The nongovernmental humanitarian aid workers, whom the US military identifies officially as "force multipliers," are seen as contributing to military goals, while US and NATO military personnel have been tasked with development and relief work. Such an approach is in direct violation of the ICRC Code of Conduct, which insists on a strict separation of humanitarian workers and NGOs from any military or political agenda and that they should work solely on the basis of need.[109]

As early as 2002 in Afghanistan, a coalition of major humanitarian aid organizations challenged the US military's strategy of assigning aid and development work to military units. The Agency Coordinating Body for Afghan Relief (ACBAR), composed of over 90 nongovermental agencies working in Afghanistan, wrote that the "military should take the necessary steps to ensure that communities, policy makers and the general public do not confuse military- and civilian-implemented assistance.... At no time should the military refer to its engagement in assistance as 'humanitarianism' or to NGOs as 'force multipliers' as both such misnomers blur the distinction between civilian- and military led interventions."[110]

By 2009, the majority of US reconstruction funding was going to the Pentagon to train, equip, and arm the Afghan army and national police. The next largest segment was for road construction serving primarily the military goal of speeding troops' access to remote areas. But roads without additional forms of economic development are little help to rural communities with no electricity and few jobs besides subsistence farming. Almost no roads in Afghanistan are safe at night. And ironically, the very roads designed to enhance military presence also enable insurgents to move swiftly from one area to another.

Construction contracts are often rife with corruption, with bribes and selective access to jobs. Military-linked construction projects can in fact serve to mobilize popular resentment toward the foreign presence and to fuel recruitment for the Taliban and other insurgents. In 2009 al-Qaeda called for the targeting of foreign civilians, including aid workers, in Afghanistan, so that the Taliban could exchange them for prisoners held by the US. The call said the US had "changed the rules of the game" by failing to distinguish between civilians and combatants and by torturing inmates.[111] Only a complete separation of development and humanitarian work from military actions will safeguard Afghan communities as well as aid workers themselves.

In August 2009 the *Washington Post* magazine documented the work of psychologists and anthropologists who joined the Pentagon's Human Terrain project, designed to provide US soldiers with better intelligence on the culture in areas of Afghanistan they were occupying. Shown in photos dressed in camouflage and armed with standard weapons, the social scientists are indistinguishable from the regular soldiers. Their effort to bring security and then development to one "model" village, Pir Zadeh in southern Afghanistan, is described thus: "They would drive in MRAPs, heavy, armored vehicles designed to minimize the effects of makeshift bombs, then would get out and move west through the village. The soldiers would create a secure perimeter as they walked... Any villager who wanted to pass the patrol would have to enter the perimeter and be frisked for weapons..." The *Post* acknowledged that few social scientists are willing to participate, but never asked the critical question of just whose village the perimeter-establishing soldiers thought it was? Though tragic, it certainly should not have surprised anyone that an earlier Human Terrain "soldier and aid worker" had been fatally attacked while she was on patrol in a neighboring village. The attacker was captured, and the aid worker's Army Ranger partner "pulled out his pistol and shot the man in the head." He pleaded guilty to man-slaughter and was sentenced to probation and a fine.[112]

What impact does the war have on the environment and agriculture?

May Kabul be without gold rather than its mountains be without snow.

—Afghan saying

Since 2002, civil organizations run by the US, the UN, and Afghanistan itself have shown concern for preserving Afghanistan's scarce natural resources. USAID is required by US law to assess the impact of projects such as dam or road construction that might disrupt Afghanistan's trickling water supply.[113] The UN Environmental Program, always attuned to resource preservation, has worked closely with the Afghan government to develop environmental regulations and helped them adopt an environmental law in January 2007. And Afghanistan's newly established National Environmental Protection Agency seeks to protect forests, watersheds, and other natural resources.

Tragically, neither US nor Afghan environmental regulations apply to military forces. No environmental assessments are done for air strikes, laying of land mines, or the storage or dumping of toxic materials at military bases. Disregard for the nation's resources over decades of war with the Soviet Union and the US and brutal cycles of droughts and floods have made many areas unlivable, destroyed the nation's agricultural sector, and crippled an economy heavily dependent on farming.

Afghanistan is a mountainous country with a very arid climate. Only about 12 percent of its land is arable and much of its agriculture relies on mountain springs and irrigation from snow melt. Yet Afghanistan was a food exporting nation up through the late 1970s. In the 1960s USAID funded construction of a dam and irrigation canals on the Helmand river by Morrison-Knudsen, the same company that built the Hoover Dam in the US. The project created 250,000 acres of arable land and involved hundreds of Afghan engineers and agronomists.

But decades of war have destroyed most of the irrigation canals in Helmand and throughout the country, ravaged what viable land existed, and planted dangerous land mines. Many of the cluster bombs used during the Afghan–Soviet war and about 10 percent of those deployed by the United

States military from 2001 through 2003 did not detonate immediately and remain scattered throughout Afghanistan as land mines. These deadly obstacles have restricted access to pastures in 81 percent of communities, to irrigated farmland in 24 percent of communities, and to rain-fed crop-land in 32 percent of communities.[114] This has devastated the agricultural sector, which supports 80 percent of the population, and the ongoing war further prevents safe land mine removal.[115] There are still 5,611 "hazards" remaining in 656 square kilometers, according to the UN Humanitarian Action Plan's Mid-Year Review for 2009.[116]

In addition to volatile land mines, detonated bombs have contaminated the soil and water supplies with "toxic compounds such as cyclonite, a carcinogen," and "rocket propellants contain[ing] perchlorates" that further harm natural resources, according to the *New Scientist*.[117]

Deforestation adds to a widening ecological crisis. A large portion of Afghanistan's forests were destroyed during conflicts with the Soviets during the 1980s and 1990s, but a combination of US military aggression and underdeveloped infra-structure continues to devastate the nation. Thirty years of war destroyed an electrical grid that had provided power to the entire city of Kabul in the 1970s, and wood remains the single largest source of energy for both heat and cooking in over 90 percent of Afghan households.

Bombing since 2001 has sparked fires and further destroyed plant life, and the "forest area declined at the rate of three percent per year from 2000 to 2005" according to the UN Environment Program.[118] Many remote mountain villages, with little arable land and no electricity to power another kind of business, rely on forests as a major source of income and fuel. As a result, President Karzai's 2006 ban on tree felling has had little effect. Forests now cover only two percent of Afghanistan.

This rapid deforestation has escalated soil erosion and contributed to the spread of disease, which makes flash flooding even more destructive for the environment and the population. In 2001, at the beginning of the war in Afghanistan, the country was suffering from a prolonged drought. With almost no regular waste removal in Kabul and other cities, dried river beds became garbage dumps. When water did return to the region it was unhampered by tree roots. As it flowed through, it depleted the soil and spread waste that contaminated water supplies. The UN reported that recent flooding affected more than 21,000 households, destroyed 17,000 acres of farmland, and killed 10,000 livestock, in addition to the untold damage of unclean water.[119]

Open drainage ditches in urban areas, which are more easily dredged when water is scarce, have also become breeding grounds for malaria. The World Health Organization lists Afghanistan as having the fourth highest incidence of malaria in the world. Contamination of wells has also contributed to high instances of diarrhea and other water-born diseases.

These environment-based humanitarian crises will only worsen in the coming years. Since the Taliban were forced out of power, refugees have flocked back to Afghanistan. An estimated 3.69 million refugees have returned, stretching already scarce natural resources like food, land mine–free farms, and water. Missing infrastructure like landfills and plumbing has also intensified the environmental impact of these refugees and will hasten the spread of disease.

Efforts to undo the military's damage to the environment are underway, but projects are poorly planned, underfunded, and slow to develop. Over the past two years the US military has sent select National Guard units as Agricultural Development Teams to specific communities to help "teach" Afghans about farming. Numerous local media— in Nebraska, Texas, Indiana, and other states where the Guard units are from—celebrate the development contributions of these units, but the impact on the ground is less clear. Such close involvement of US military with farmers risks militarizing agriculture, and the notion that soldiers can teach farmers about farming is at best highly inefficient and at worst incredibly patronizing.

The National Agricultural Development Framework and the comprehensive Agricultural and Rural Development Facility are joint efforts of the Afghan government, the UN, and the World Bank that also aim to redevelop agriculture by providing incentives for farmers to plant wheat and other crops in place of poppies. Yet funding for agricultural development is dwarfed by military spending. With widespread corruption in national ministries, many Afghans distrust these large-scale national projects.

By contrast, some Afghan and international NGOs are working with local communities to plant orchards and create small farming cooperatives. Yet most of these cooperatives are small scale and orchards takes several years to become viable.

It will take time for Afghanistan and the global community to undo the damage caused by decades of war, and the ongoing "war on terror" is counter-productive to any mission to improve Afghanistan's environment. So long as military conflict continues, these small-scale efforts will be overshadowed by violence and destruction, and the Afghan people will suffer from a lack of resources. Only an international effort unhampered by counter-productive military operations can restore Afghanistan's prosperity.

What is the connection between war and drugs in Afghanistan?

There is a long and close relationship between drugs and war in Afghanistan. As in Southeast Asia during the Vietnam War, the longstanding civil war in Colombia, and other zones of conflict, the Afghan drug trade is closely linked with the arms trade. The production of illegal drugs provides a ready source of cash to fund arms deals for local warlords and militias. Large sums of drug money also facilitate a climate of rampant corruption and bribes among government officials.

In 1994 Mahbub ul Haq, the founder of the UN Human Development report, drew significant parallels between the global arms trade and the global drug trade. He noted that when it comes to the "war on drugs," governments of the North have long argued that the primary problem is the suppliers of drugs (mostly from impoverished, war-torn countries of the global South). Yet when it comes to the global arms trade, the problem, these same Northern governments say, is the consumers (mostly governments and armed groups in the impoverished, war-torn global South). Both those strategies have failed. The Human Development report documents how both the arms trade and drug trade have contributed tremendously to widening human insecurity. For thirty years the flood of arms imports and drug exports has wrought havoc in the lives of most Afghans.

Beginning in the 1980s when the Soviet army controlled Afghanistan, Mujahideen fighting groups found opium production an easy source of cash to buy increasingly sophisticated weapons. From 1979 through the early 1990s, the CIA, Saudi Arabia, and Pakistan were also funneling weapons to the same Mujahideen groups involved in opium production. Despite the US administration's "war on drugs," when it came to Afghanistan, the drug dealers were our friends.

Poor farmers could make many times more money from poppy production than from any other crop. Though few farmers would cultivate poppies as their main crop, many found growing poppies on a portion of their land a lucrative endeavor. Other farmers were forced by warlords to produce poppies as a kind of security payment. Annual surveys show that poppy production escalated dramatically during the 1980s. In 1985 opium production nearly tripled to 400 metric tons from 140 tons just a year earlier. With a weak central government, local warlords profited dramatically from the growing opium trade.

Once the Soviet military withdrew in 1989, and the US stopped shipping arms to various Mujahideen fighters in 1991, opium became even more important as a source of funding for warlords that had taken to fighting one another for control of Afghanistan.

When the Taliban seized control of Kabul in 1996 there was little change in the amount of opium production, despite their opposition to drug use. Production and sales continued. But in 2001 the Taliban decided to clamp down on poppy production and in one year reduced production from 3,278 metric tons in 2000, to only 185 tons just one year later. It was perhaps the most successful drug eradication program in world history. But the Taliban did not stop drug traffickers from selling existing stocks of opium. Nor did they stop collecting an *ushr* (a tax of roughly 10 percent) on ongoing opium sales. Since the previous several years had yielded bumper crops, the price of heroin had fallen. With the Taliban clampdown, prices soared and they were still able to profit from existing supplies.

Local farmers, however, found themselves deeply indebted to drug dealers, with no means of paying off these debts. Growing resentment among many farmers found welcome relief when the US and Northern Alliance toppled the Taliban in the fall of 2001—just as poppy season was beginning in November.

Since the US invasion in late 2001, poppy cultivation has exploded exponentially. From the 185 tons in 2001, opium production catapulted to 3,400 tons in 2002. As the US administration turned its attention to invading Iraq starting in

2002, it did not want to become involved in a "war on drugs" in Afghanistan. Secretary of Defense Donald Rumsfeld and other officials even declared that any efforts at stopping the drug trade would take away from their goal of hunting al-Qaeda and other terrorists.

In 2004 production reached 4,200 tons. In 2006 it rose again and in 2007 it peaked at 8,200 tons. These rapid increases meant hundreds of millions of dollars in the hands of armed groups. Some were members of the Afghan parliament or in Afghan ministries. Others included the Taliban and other opposition groups. It is estimated that one third to half of the gross domestic product of Afghanistan comes from drugs each year. These massive amounts have fueled widening corruption, instability, and violence throughout the country.

In 2008 opium production declined slightly. In part the decline was due to global food prices rising dramatically. Alternative crops such as wheat became much more profitable than in previous years. A drought also reduced production.

Since the US/NATO occupation of Afghanistan began, the variety of efforts by US, NATO, and the Afghan government at reducing the drug trade have failed dismally. There are three main strategies: poppy eradication, interdiction that targets drug traffickers and dealers, and development programs offering alternative livelihoods for farmers. When the US began to stress eradication programs, it strongly proposed using aerial fumigations similar to ones used widely in Colombia. One top US official recently stated, "The more Afghanistan can look like Colombia, the better." Aerial sprayings use US-manufactured herbicides. Spraying can cover wide areas but also cause many health and environmental risks to those living in the affected areas.

The Afghan government and many NATO countries opposed fumigations and instead suggested eradication on the ground combined with economic alternatives. Such methods are slower and more labor intensive. Manual eradication poses greater risks of armed attacks on those destroying the fields, yet does not cause indiscriminate harm to people, livestock, other crops, and water sources.

Ironically, drug traffickers have not always opposed eradication programs. These programs keep prices up, keep attention away from traffickers' own role in the drug trade, and mobilize community opposition to the government. Because such a campaign might increase grassroots support for the Taliban, Gretchen Peters, in her book *Seeds of Terror: How Heroin is Bankrolling the Taliban and al Qaeda*, speculates, "Perhaps the Taliban are still hoping the Obama administration will go ahead with an aerial spraying campaign."[120] Armed groups easily turn to another source for poppies when a field is destroyed. Eradication programs target the fields of farmers before poppies are harvested. Poor farmers widely oppose any eradication programs.

Interdiction efforts are expensive and ineffective as the traffickers they target are highly mobile, heavily armed, and have huge sums of money for bribes.

Most of the funding for eradication and interdiction goes to military forces. Alternative livelihood programs require redirecting government funds from militarized programs to poor farmers and their communities. Strong local and provincial leadership, combined with funding for viable economic alternatives for farmers, has all but eliminated opium production in several provinces like Nangarhar and Balkh for the moment. Yet simply reducing opium production is not a measure of success. While increasing grain prices helped some farmers, it squeezed other families who lacked land or work. A December 2008 Afghanistan Research and Evaluation Unit (AREU) report entitled "Counter-Narcotics in Afghanistan: The Failure of Success?" observed, "Sustainable reductions in opium poppy culti-vation will only be achieved by a wider process of improved security, economic growth and governance, rather than by a distinct and parallel set of more limited counter-narcotics activities."[121]

For years Helmand has produced the bulk of Afghan's poppies. In 2008, estimates were that Helmand and four other southern provinces accounted for 98 percent of poppy cultivation. Helmand alone accounted for over half. When the Taliban clamped down in 2001, it created tremendous economic hardship for many farmers in Helmand and fueled resentment against Taliban rule. Farmers had many accumulated debts and saw poppy production as the only means to pay off these debts.

In 2006, Helmand became the locus of British military efforts. In 2009 the US troop escalation brought thousands more foreign troops into the province. The US military presence seriously challenges a major source of funds for the Taliban if those troops curtail poppy production. Yet such a move will severely impact Helmand and other local farmers for whom a major source of income will be cut off without any viable alternative.

One reason farmers keep turning to poppy production is the years of armed conflict. Constant war has destroyed crops but also created widespread insecurity on roads. It is both dangerous and expensive (due to numerous checkpoints where armed groups collect bribes) to get wheat, fruits, or any other perishable product to market. With poppies, the traffickers will come to farmers. For many farmers, poppy crops are not only more lucrative but safer for themselves and their families.

The AREU report concludes, "the predatory behavior of corrupt officials and the proliferation of checkpoints and 'nuisance taxes' have returned. Consequently, the cost of traveling one kilometer in the south is three times that of traveling the same distance in the eastern, central or northern regions, making transporting legal agricultural crops to market cost-prohibitive."[122]

Perhaps because of the bitter lesson of failure in earlier "drug wars," US drug policy in Afghanistan seems to have rejected the Colombia model of focusing on airborne eradication campaigns, and instead is considering an emphasis on going after traffickers and at least beginning alternative production projects.

What is the difference between counterterrorism and counterinsurgency?

Much has been made of the Obama administration's claims that its Afghanistan strategy is no longer based on counterterrorism, but instead on counter-insurgency. To military strategists, "counter-insurgency operations are aimed primarily at influencing the population and are primarily non-military, counter-terrorism operations are exclusively military and focus on targeting the 'enemy.'"[123] The Obama administration's definition is not that clear.

The administration claims that it has moved strategically in Afghanistan, leaving behind the ineffective counterterrorism approach of the Bush administration and replacing it with a more nuanced and "better" counterinsurgency strategy. The shift was symbolized by the abrupt firing of Afghanistan commander General David Mac-Kiernon and his replacement with General Stanley McChrystal. The claimed distinction lay primarily in abandoning the earlier counterterrorism strategy that was based on finding and killing as many "enemy" opponents as possible. That strategy would be replaced with an effort to protect the Afghan people (that is, protect them from the Taliban or other anti-US forces, not from the consequences of the US war), ostensibly by winning their hearts and minds.

The theoretical logic was clear: if your priority is to protect civilians, rather than to kill as many opponents as possible, you are much more likely to win support from the local population. But that theoretical logic leaves many questions when applied to the real world. The US counter-insurgency effort to "protect" Afghans, known as "clear, hold and build," remains grounded in fighting and killing insurgents, whether Taliban or other armed opposition groups. In fact "clear," the first step, refers directly to "clearing" an area of armed opponents of the US and its Afghan allies—in many cases without consultation with local Afghans. But although Taliban leaders were sometimes successfully targeted, large numbers of civilians have been killed in many, perhaps most, of those attacks. So even if the goal is to win popular support from Afghan civilians, even for those who oppose the Taliban, the "clear" part of the strategy is already problematic.

Although the new strategy announced in spring 2009 officially emphasized protecting civilians, its operations have continued to put civilians at risk of attack by US air strikes (even if somewhat less frequently than before), by crossfire between US and opposition forces, by roadside bombs or other attacks meant for US or US-backed government troops, and by Taliban and other insurgent forces who punish those believed to support the US and its allies.

McChrystal's rise to command was based on the claim that he represented a new kind of military strategist, uniquely able to lead US forces into battle in Afghanistan. He would focus not on tracking down and killing the enemy, but on this ostensibly new strategy of winning hearts and minds and protecting civilians. But McChrystal's own history belies that claim. His earlier experience, beginning with his days in Vietnam, was in old-fashioned "get the bad guys" counter-terrorism. More recently, he spent most of the five years before his promotion in Afghanistan and surrounding countries, where he commanded special forces units focused on the pursuit of individual al-Qaeda and other insurgent leaders in Afghanistan, Iraq, and Pakistan. That meant primarily air strikes and targeted raids, the traditional methods of counterterrorism. He worked closely with Bush-era Secretary of Defense Donald Rumsfeld, who viewed McChrystal's special operations team as his own counterweight to the CIA, and authorized them to "conduct global operations against terrorist networks" unilaterally anywhere in the world.[124]

In fact, contrary to the notion that McChrystal's command would focus on protecting Afghan civilians, senior Pentagon officials acknowledge that "Escalating violence, an acceleration of targeted killings, and deniable attacks by US Special Forces on Taliban strong holds in Pakistan will all be the major results of the administration's latest change in command in Afghanistan." According to Richard Sale, defense correspondent for the *Middle East Times*, those Pentagon sources warned that McChrystal's appointment "portends a much bloodier phase of the war.... 'McChrystal is an expert killer. That's what the teams he heads are good at,' said former senior DIA official Pat Lang. 'The idea is to put out the eyes of the insurgency using force,' a Pentagon official said."[125]

The inadequacy of a counterinsurgency campaign in Afghanistan, and the likelihood that it will fail, is due to more than the choice of McChrystal. Overall US counterinsurgency strategy is based on the counterinsurgency field manual that was published in 2006 and written by General David Petraeus, head of the Pentagon's Central Command, which oversees both Afghanistan and Iraq. But the applicability of those guidelines to Afghanistan remain problematic. According to one military analyst at the University of Alabama, US strategy as outlined by the manual

> fails to recognize that the outsider COINs [counter-insurgent forces] are probably part of the problem as well as the solution. Foreign forces, no matter how well intentioned are, after all, foreigners, and their presence is not going to be universally appreciated, either by those who are suspicious of foreigners (which includes most Afghans) and those whose causes are harmed by their presence. Moreover, the need to invite foreigners in to defeat the insurgents says something basically negative about the HN (host nation) government being helped (e.g. if the government was doing its job, why would it need foreign assistance?). Moreover, those who collaborate with the outsiders are going to be viewed by some as, well, collaborators, and the presence of those troops will in turn help insurgent recruitment.

So the question remains whether US-style counterinsurgency is any more likely to bring "victory" in Afghanistan than eight years of a failed counterterrorism strategy. The same military analyst argues no. First, Afghanistan is too big—US strategy requires twenty "counterinsurgents" for every thousand people in the population to be protected—that would mean a minimum of 660,000 troops. Second, the strategy requires political conversion of the population—but with no clarity about who might do the converting—"if it leaves this to US counter-insurgents, the battle is lost." This includes the need for "a good government the population can be loyal to. It is not at all clear Afghanistan has or is in any danger of acquiring such a government." Third, counterinsurgency wars take a long time, a decade or more. Will the American public, he asks, "support an Afghanistan war still going on in 2018 or 2019? I doubt it."[126]

PART V

The War in Afghanistan Goes Global

What roles do NATO and other countries play in the war?

The war in Afghanistan has from the beginning been led by the US, but backed by a shifting coalition that has included roles for NATO, the United Nations, and a host of individual countries. Ultimate control, however, has never left US hands.

Within 24 hours of the September 11 attacks, the Bush administration won commitments of support for war in Afghanistan from Britain's prime minister, Tony Blair, and from Pakistan's military ruler, General Pervez Musharraf. Also on September 12, the North Atlantic Treaty Organization announced its intention to use, for the first time, Article V of the NATO Charter, which states that an attack on any NATO member will be treated as an attack on all. On October 2 NATO formally invoked Article V, putting the military alliance on a war footing.

George W. Bush demanded that the Taliban turn over Osama bin Laden to the US for trial. The Taliban refused. At noon on October 7, 2001, the Taliban's ambassador to Pakistan, Abdul Salam Zaeef, offered to "detain bin Laden and try him under Islamic law if the United States makes a formal request and presents them with evidence." The Bush administration rejected the offer, and three hours later launched a massive air assault against Afghanistan.

The day before, Deputy Secretary of State Richard Armitage had claimed that an international coalition was in place to begin military action. "We've got many countries who have actively sought us in order to engage in military activities with us. We've got overflight rights from over 26 countries, and we've got basing agreements with about 21 countries right now," he said.[127] But when Washington's planes and submarines sent their missiles into Afghanistan on October 7, its only operational partner was Great Britain.

Many governments did express public support for the US war. The US was able to rely on airbases in Uzbekistan and Tajikistan because Russian President Vladimir Putin agreed in the first week after 9/11 to facilitate the arrangement. Saudi Arabia and the UAE both cut their diplomatic ties to the Taliban, leaving Pakistan as the only country maintaining official relations. The US did not press the issue with its ally in Islamabad. In fact, looking to shore up South Asian support for its looming war, just days after 9/11 Washington dropped the sanctions it had imposed on both Pakistan and India as punishment for the two countries' nuclear bomb tests in 1998.

Throughout the first months of the US air war in Afghanistan, only Britain joined in. Other countries, including France, Germany, Australia, and Italy, promised to send troops, but did not enter the fray. Under the pressure of US–UK bombs and missile strikes as well as the US ground troops, the Taliban scattered, its control of Kabul and other cities largely disappearing. The Northern Alliance, whose Russian- and Indian-backed guerrilla supporters were mainly ethnic Tajik and Uzbek Afghans, came in out of the cold, becoming the official allies of the US, and by mid-November 2001 they took over Kabul.

In the meantime, even before the US–UK bombing began, representatives of the Northern Alliance met in Rome with the exiled King of Afghanistan, Zahir Shah, whom many believed could serve as a unifying figure for a new national government in Kabul. They agreed to participate in a conference to establish an interim government, to be made up of tribal and militia leaders. On November 10, Bush addressed the United Nations General Assembly, with a bellicose speech in which he threatened that "We must unite in opposing all terrorists... Any government that rejects this principle, trying to pick and choose its terrorist friends, will know the consequences."[128]

In early December the Afghanistan conference was convened in Bonn, ostensibly at the invitation of the UN. The Afghan participants were diverse in ethnicity, language, politics, and goals, and united only in their opposition to the Taliban. The United States, however, exerted enough control over the agenda and participation that the US-backed candidate to become chairman of the new interim authority, Hamid Karzai, was quickly chosen. The UN representative, the brilliant and experienced Algerian diplomat Lakhdar Brahimi, admitted that "the Americans in general were really then putting the pressure."[129]

The Bonn agreement also called on the UN to create an International Security Assistance Force (ISAF). The initial UN mandate limited the role of the British-led ISAF to providing security in Kabul alone. Other European countries, both members and non-members of NATO, joined ISAF (including Turkey, which was significant because it was the first Muslim-majority country to join the military coalition). Other countries outside of Europe joined as well, in most cases in hopes of greater support, aid, or credibility from the Bush administration. Those countries include Australia, Jordan, New Zealand, the Philippines, Singapore, South Korea, and the United Arab Emirates.

A year and a half after its creation, in August 2003, ISAF was turned over to NATO's strategic command; it was the first time NATO as an alliance sent ground forces outside of Europe. When NATO took command of ISAF, it also began expanding the mission of ISAF to provide security in all of Afghanistan, not only the capital.

As of the spring of 2009, NATO claimed that

its 50,000 troops come from 41 different countries, including all 26 NATO members.[130] But problems of unilateral control remain. The same US general serves simultaneously as commander of the NATO forces (which include some US troops) and of the separate US unilateral forces in Afghanistan. Tensions rise since the US, and to a lesser degree Britain, continue to demand that more troops from other NATO countries be sent to Afghanistan, while other coalition countries are actually downsizing their troop deployments. Additionally, participating countries within NATO differ as to what their role should be in Afghanistan. With the US and Britain, as well as Canada, the Netherlands, and a few others focusing on the military goals of the so-called global war on terror, other coalition countries, including Germany, Italy, and others, prioritize the need for stability and reconstruction in Afghanistan.[131] This has led to serious divides within the alliance, as many national contingents in Afghanistan, including those of Germany and Italy are prohibited from participating in major combat or counterinsurgency activities. While these countries still function as military forces, and most have experienced casualties among their troops, their mandates are largely limited to rebuilding and other non-combat missions.

Since 2003, when ISAF's mission was expanded to include security in all of Afghanistan, its operations have been generally carried out by "Provincial Reconstruction Teams" or PRTs. These teams, ostensibly joint civilian–military partnerships, are in fact controlled by the military command structure, and have the dangerous effect of militarizing the provision of humanitarian aid to Afghanistan. This endangers the crucial perception of aid workers and humanitarian organizations as neutral, and ultimately puts Afghans' access to desperately needed assistance at risk. (See page 102.)

With the inauguration of President Barack Obama, supporting the escalating US war became even somewhat easier for other governments, although many continued their trajectory toward pulling all their troops out of Afghanistan. By July 2009, the once-hesitant Russia agreed to provide direct road access for US troops into Afghanistan. Three months later China announced that its military had begun training Afghan (and Iraqi) officers in mine clearance.[132]

But the divide within the US-backed coalition and within NATO in particular continues. As *New York Times* columnist Thomas Friedman wrote in the first few months of the Afghanistan war, "we are increasingly headed for a military apartheid within NATO: America will be the chef who decides the menu and cooks all the great meals, and the NATO allies will be the busboys who stay around and clean up the mess and keep the peace—indefinitely."[133]

NATO governments are under increasing domestic pressure to withdraw their troops from the quagmire of Afghanistan, so that apartheid divide will only continue to grow. By the summer of 2009, public opposition to the war in Afghanistan in key NATO allied countries was rising again. In the UK, 60 percent said they wanted the troops to leave Afghanistan. In Italy, 55 percent opposed their troop deployment even before the deaths of six Italian soldiers on September 17, 2009; the percentage rose further after that event. In Germany, 60 percent of the population think their country's role in the war is a mistake. That could explain the kind of national denial one German analyst described, in which people "don't call it a war… as if we had sent 4,000 social workers" to Afghanistan in the NATO deployment.[134]

That "apartheid divide" was part of the reason that eight years of war had failed. As Lakhdar Brahimi, who had organized the Bonn conference on behalf of the UN in 2001, said in 2009,

> What has been missing these past few years is a common strategy for all who are involved in Afghanistan. What we've had until now were different national policies. It was not a division of labor; it was different agendas. That is ineffective and at times disastrous because, obviously, it is not possible for several countries to wage separate wars in the same country and be successful.[135]

What role has the United Nations played in Afghanistan since 9/11?

By the end of its first months in office, the George W. Bush administration had already succeeded in antagonizing much of the membership of the United Nations. By May 2001 unabashed uni-lateralism, the "unsigning" of multilateral treaties, and open disregard for the UN led to the US being voted out of the UN Human Rights Commission. By July, *New York Times* columnist Thomas Friedman lamented how "America is referred to as a 'rogue state' in Europe now as often as Iraq."[136]

All of that was reversed, at least temporarily, on September 11. Called into emergency session just 24 hours after the attacks, the UN Security Council's shaken diplomats voted unanimously to pass Reso-lution 1368, drafted by the US delegation. With virtually global solidarity with the people of the US, there was no question that the Council, at that moment, would have unanimously passed anything the US requested. But the US did not ask the Security Council to authorize the use of force, as the UN Charter requires (see page 19) for any military action to be deemed legitimate. This was the first indication of the US's intention to launch a war on its own terms, with international assistance only under Washington's firm control.

On the same day, the UN pulled its inter-national staff out of Afghanistan, clearly understanding what lay ahead for the country. Three weeks into the US air assault, the UN reported an imminent humanitarian catastrophe, and resumed humanitarian aid, carried out entirely by Afghan staff. When the US-backed Northern Alliance guerrilla force occupied Kabul after the Taliban fled the capital, they asked the UN to participate in consultations among various Afghan factions aimed at establishing a new government.

In the late autumn of 2001, as the fall of the Taliban seemed imminent, the US pushed the UN to take the lead in pulling together a meeting of ostensibly representative Afghan personalities to plan for the creation of a new government. The mandate of the gathering was to arrange for a loya jirga, or grand council, to be held in Afghanistan to provide legitimacy for a government that the Bonn meeting would select. The experienced Algerian diplomat and longtime UN troubleshooter Lakhdar Brahimi, was designated the UN's representative to arrange and run the meeting.

After just days of meeting, the Bonn accord was signed. It created an interim administration to run for six months, which would then be responsible for convening the loya jirga to establish a follow-up transitional government that would organize general elections. But from the beginning it was clear the meeting's real goal was to ensure that the government in post-Taliban Afghanistan would be led by Afghans chosen by and accountable to Washington and its allies. Years later Brahimi acknowledged:

> we are now paying the price for what we did wrong from day one. First, the people who were in Bonn were not fully representative of the rich variety of the Afghan people. I underlined this fact to the thirty-five delegates we brought together in Bonn again and again. I made the point once more when an agreement was reached and we all prepared to return to Kabul: the popular base of the interim administration put together in Bonn under President Karzai was far too narrow. We all vowed to work hard to widen that base once we returned to Kabul. Unfortunately, very little was done. On the contrary, the Northern Alliance, which had been thoroughly defeated by the Taliban and had been literally resuscitated from certain death by the US was actively engaged in consolidating its grip over the country.[137]

By the middle of December, with the US-backed Hamid Karzai safely ensconced as interim president in Kabul, the UN Security Council authorized the creation of the International Security Assistance Force (ISAF), under overall US control but with a British commander on the ground. The UN resolution authorized ISAF troops to use force if necessary, but a British military official at the time said the force would be only "lightly" armed, and described its mission as a "peace support operation." Afghanistan's newly appointed Interim Defense Minister Mohammed Fahim said the ISAF troops would *not* have authority to disarm belligerents, interfere in Afghan affairs, or use force.

Once the resolution was passed, however, the United Nations was essentially written out of the strategic picture. ISAF remained under overall US control, with a small percentage of US troops in Afghanistan operating within ISAF, the majority remaining under direct US military command. And the UN mandate authorized ISAF to function only in and around the capital, Kabul.

A few years later, when the UN met to expand ISAF's jurisdiction to the whole of Afghanistan, the command of the "UN force" was formally handed over to NATO. On March 30, 2003, just days after the US invasion of Iraq, the ISAF command center in Kabul, officially the UN headquarters, came under rocket-fire attack.[138] While there were no casualties, the attack was seen by many as an indication that the UN, by operating in Afghanistan in what appeared to be an alliance with an already unpopular foreign military occupation, was already paying a heavy price for its involvement in the US-led war. Five months later in Iraq, a deadly attack on UN headquarters at the Canal Hotel in Baghdad was widely understood to be the horrifying consequence of UN involvement in the illegal war there.

Twenty-two UN staff members were killed, including the special representative of the secretary-general, Sergio Vieira de Mello.

While Afghanistan remained at war and under military occupation, the UN presence there was supposed to be focused on elections and economic and development assistance. But despite extensive fundraising and development efforts, the UN was constrained by the lack of security throughout the country and by the priority the wealthy countries, especially the US, gave to military spending over development commitments. As to the election process, by the time the August 2009 elections were approaching, the US and NATO were both ramping up large numbers of troops to deploy across the country. The UN played a significant role in laying the political groundwork for that poll. But the challenge of voter security, and the related question of whether any election held under the conditions of a massive foreign military occupation could ever be deemed free and fair, continued to dominate. On those questions, the UN remained largely silent.

Less than a week before the second round of the election was scheduled, the UN faced a new challenge, its first direct attack in Afghanistan. Five international UN staff were killed, and others injured, in an assault on their residence in Kabul on October 28, 2009. The Taliban claimed responsibility.

For many, it was horrifyingly reminiscent of the truck bomb attack of August 2003, when the UN's Iraq headquarters in Baghdad was blown up, killing the 22 staff members. On both occasions, UN staff paid the price for their organization being one-sided—working with and on the side of a corrupt government and foreign troops in an occupied country—and thus viewed as siding with the occupation.

What has Pakistan's role been in the war?

The fact that the Obama administration uses the term "Af-Pak" to describe not only its theater of war but also its strategic approach, is a clear indication of the centrality of Pakistan within the US war. During the first months of Obama's presidency the US significantly escalated the air war in Pakistan against the Pakistani Taliban, including the use of drone air strikes, with a resulting rise in civilian casualties and anti-US sentiment.

There is little question that the top leadership of al-Qaeda is not in Afghanistan at all, but rather is based primarily in the rugged mountain regions of Pakistan near the Afghan border. While Afghanistan is identified as a strategic target for the US mostly because of the claimed fear that a return to Taliban control would allow al-Qaeda to rebuild safe havens in Afghanistan, Pakistan is much more important in its own right. Many people believe

the US is continuing the war against Afghanistan
because it is impossible to imagine a full-scale war
against the much larger population of a nuclear-
armed Pakistan next door.

The links between the US, Pakistan, the Taliban
in Afghanistan, and al-Qaeda are complex. Pakistan's
military has longstanding ties to the US and depends
on the US for military aid that has amounted to
more than $10 billion since 9/11.[139] Washington
remains the main backer of the Pakistani military,
viewing it as much stronger than the civilian
government and the only viable institution in a very
unstable country with an arsenal of nuclear weapons
and in a strategic neighborhood.

But the Pakistani government does not share
all US interests in their country. In fact the two
governments' interests often collide. The US wants
the Pakistani military to go after and destroy all
Taliban and al-Qaeda sanctuaries in Pakistan. But
the authorities in Pakistan don't see things the same
way, since the Pakistani Taliban, while a problem, is
not nearly as strong relative to the Pakistani government as the separate Afghan Taliban is in relation to
the very weak Afghan government. Pakistan's
strategic fear is of India, not the Taliban. So Pakistan
has long been a key backer of the Afghan Taliban,
seeing it as a bulwark against the India-backed
government and tribal militia forces in neighboring
Afghanistan. Islamabad's priority is eliminating the

Pakistani Taliban and other militant groups that disrupt government control of the country. The Pakistani government has little interest in attacking the Afghan Taliban forces that are fighting against the US on both sides of the border, but are not particularly a threat to itself. To complicate matters even further, Pakistan has used some of the groups associated with the Pakistani Taliban as proxy fighters against India in the ongoing Kashmir conflict.[140]

So both the Bush and later Obama administrations largely failed to persuade the Pakistani government to go after the Afghan Taliban on the Pakistan side of the border. Only later, when the Pentagon made it a priority to do what the Pakistani government wanted, which was to target the Pakistani Taliban with drone attacks (the CIA famously found and killed Pakistani Taliban leader Baitullah Mehsud in a missile attack in August 2009[141]), did US hopes begin to rise that Pakistan would pay more attention to the anti-US Afghan Taliban fighters.

The price of that direct US military involvement, of course, was an increase in civilian casualties. Despite the widespread antagonism toward President George Bush throughout the region, President Obama's increasing use of drone attacks in Pakistan (even while they were somewhat reduced in Afghanistan) created even greater anger.

By the summer of 2009, a Gallup poll in Pakistan indicated that while 11 percent of the population viewed Taliban fighters as the biggest threat, and 18 percent assigned that role to India, a full 59 percent of respondents said that the greatest threat facing Pakistan was the United States itself.[142]

Under US as well as domestic pressure, the Pakistani military has moved against local extremist forces, including the Pakistani Taliban when the latter moved down from the mountains to confront major population centers—as in May 2009 in the Swat Valley. (The army has not moved as decisively in the mountainous tribal areas.) But the results have been dire. More than 2.4 million people were forced to flee the military offensive in the Swat Valley, the largest refugee crisis in the region since the Bangladesh crisis of 1971. Many or most of the displaced people returned home within a few months. But according to the *New York Times*, "two months after the Pakistani Army wrested control of the Swat Valley from Taliban militants, a new campaign of fear has taken hold, with scores, perhaps hundreds, of bodies dumped on the streets in what human rights advocates and local residents say is the work of the military."[143]

The Pakistani military has long been involved in problematic activities. In the 1980s its ISI (Inter-Services Intelligence) agency was the key conduit for US arms and Saudi money to Afghanistan's anti-

Soviet Mujahideen, and in the 1990s it was a key backer of the Afghan Taliban. But there is little evidence to back up the often-heard claim that the ISI operates as an independent, even rogue agency; in fact it is part of the military structure and answers to the military command.[144] It is unlikely the Pakistani military wants or would be willing to take on sustained actions against armed groups in Pakistani territory near the Afghan border, if those groups were not threatening the Pakistani state. It's an open question whether the military and/or the Pakistani government, let alone the majority of the Pakistani population, would be prepared to accept greater influence of Islamist forces within bigger population centers, in return for the armed groups not challenging Islamabad's authority. According to a summer 2009 Gallup poll, about 43 percent of Pakistanis support dialogue with the Taliban.[145]

The costs of the war in Pakistan are enormous. The vast majority of Pakistanis remain impoverished; the country ranks 173rd in per capita GDP.[146] Yet both US aid allocations and the Pakistani government's budget privilege military and security spending rather than education, clean water, healthcare, jobs, etc. The common call from US military and political officials for an "80–20" split in Afghanistan spending, with 80 percent for development and social needs and only 20 percent for military, is not often heard when discussing

Pakistan. The result is that the country remains unstable, highly militarized, and very poor.

What role has Iran played in Afghanistan since 9/11?

Like every government in the world, Iran's leaders condemned the September 11 terrorist attacks. Iran's then President Khatami called the attacks "the ugliest form of terrorism ever seen."[147] Despite the ongoing US sanctions in place against Iran, Khatami's government offered to assist the US and other Western countries in stabilizing Afghanistan after the overthrow of the Taliban government. The offer reflected longstanding Iranian opposition to the Taliban, but also a remarkable openness to cooperation with the US. Some in Washington seemed to find it difficult to take Iran's offer seriously, but for diplomats on the ground it worked. According to James Dobbins, Bush's first post-9/11 envoy to Afghanistan, Iran's assistance to the US in Afghanistan in the months after the attacks represented "perhaps the most constructive period of US–Iranian diplomacy since the fall of the shah of Iran." According to Dobbins:

> Many believe that in the wake of Sept. 11, the United States formed an international coalition and toppled the Taliban. It would be more accurate to say that the United States joined a coalition that had been battling the Taliban for

nearly a decade. This coalition—made up of Iran, India, Russia and the Northern Alliance, and aided by massive American airpower—drove the Taliban from power. The coalition then worked closely with the United States to secure agreement among all elements of the Afghan opposition on the formation of a broadly based successor to the Taliban regime.

As the American representative at the U.N. conference in Bonn, Germany, where this agreement was reached, I worked closely with the Iranian delegation and others. Iranian representatives were particularly helpful. It was, for instance, the Iranian delegate who first insisted that the agreement include a commitment to hold democratic elections in Afghanistan. This same Iranian persuaded the Northern Alliance to make the essential concession that allowed the meeting to conclude successfully.[148]

Iran's involvement in the anti-Taliban coalition, acknowledged by Dobbins, was reaffirmed by Iran's own leaders. In 2005, Mohsen Rezaie, then head of the Revolutionary Guards (who ran for president in Iran's disputed 2009 election), said the US had not given Iran enough credit for what he said was Iran's "important role in the overthrow of the Taliban" in 2001. He said that Revolutionary Guard troops actually advised and fought with the Northern Alliance forces, including playing a key role in the capture of Kabul. US troops and officials confirmed that Iranians were present with the

Northern Alliance at the time.[149]

But Iranian cooperation in Washington's invasion and occupation of Afghanistan and its political aftermath were apparently not enough to satisfy the Bush administration. Just a few weeks after Iran backed the inauguration of the US-backed Hamid Karzai as president of occupied Afghanistan, Bush's January 2002 State of the Union address identified Iran as part of the so-called axis of evil. In August, Iran's President Khatami became the first head of state to visit Afghanistan since the overthrow of the Taliban. Just a few months later, Bush suspended all bilateral contacts with Iran.

The US/NATO occupation of Afghanistan and US backing of the government there did not, however, prevent the resumption of trade and economic ties between Iran and post-Taliban Afghanistan. Since 2003 Iran has been a major partner for Afghanistan's struggling economy, partly because President Hamid Karzai remained wary of Pakistan, another traditional Afghan trading partner, and partly because of Islamabad's long-standing support for the Taliban.[150]

Over the next several years relations between Afghanistan and Iran continued to expand, despite rising tension between Iran and the US. By 2005 the head of defense analysis at London's International Institute for Strategic Studies was quoted by Radio Free Europe, a US government-

controlled outlet, acknowledging Iran's role in
Afghanistan's future reconstruction and development. Iran and Afghanistan "are being closely linked
by efforts against the Taliban in the past," Colonel
Christopher Langton said, "but also because of the
influence that Iran can bring there with the Hazara
population [who, like Iranians, are Shi'a Muslims].
And in the development sector, there are already
projects which Iran is involved in... There is a
whole list of political, economic, and security issues
which connect Afghanistan and Iran."

Those developments were taking place
simultaneously with a major escalation in US
threats against Iran. Indeed, in the same Radio Free
Europe interview, a spokesman for the Afghan
government's defense ministry had to deny a report
that US military special operations forces had
infiltrated Iran from Afghanistan.[151]

With the election of President Obama, the new
administration's parallel commitments to engagement with Iran and escalation in Afghanistan took
shape simultaneously. Within weeks of Obama's
2009 inauguration, just as the White House was
announcing its new strategy for the war in Afghanistan, US and Iranian diplomats gathered in Moscow
for discussions. Russia's Foreign Minister Sergei
Lavror noted, "We've turned a page to have Iranians
and Americans at the same table all discussing
Afghanistan."[152] No far-reaching commitments were

made at that meeting, but the long-standing relations—economic and political—between Iran and Afghanistan continue.

—PART VI—

Ending the War

Is there a military solution in Afghanistan?

In asymmetrical, guerrilla warfare as in Afghanistan, no amounts of sophisticated weaponry, no amounts of military funding or increases in troops will bring peace. Years of foreigners pumping billions of arms into Afghanistan have instead yielded a destroyed infrastructure as well as a country divided by tribal allegiances, an economy reliant on foreign aid and drugs, a government known for its oppression of women. Reflecting on the second Anglo–Afghan War during the 1880s, Rudyard Kipling penned the poem, "The Accidental Frontier" as a lesson to imperial military leaders, that highly trained foreign soldiers are no match for indigenous resistance movements, however poor:

> Two thousand pounds of education
> Drops to a ten-rupee jezail
> Strike hard who cares, shoot straight who can
> The odds are on the cheaper man.

So far, the US is repeating the errors of past would-be nation builders.

As General David Petraeus, US commander for Iraq and Afghanistan, admitted, "As important as they are in achieving security, military actions by themselves cannot achieve success in counter-insurgency. Insurgents that never defeat counter-insurgents in combat still may achieve their strategic objectives."[153]

As the violence and casualties of wars in both Afghanistan and Iraq escalated in 2006, the US military began rethinking its strategies. When General Petraeus, author of the new US Army manual on counterinsurgency, assumed command, he quickly made public a shift in strategy in Iraq that became known as "the surge." The 2007 troop surge in Iraq led political leaders to mistakenly claim that military success in stabilizing Iraq was linked almost exclusively to troop levels, while ignoring other factors such as massive payouts (bribes) to Sunni militia to stop fighting the US. Now similar arguments are being claimed regarding Afghanistan: that an escalation of US and international troops, combined with an escalation in the number of trained Afghan army and police forces, will somehow provide the military solution that so far has eluded the US and coalition forces.

General Petraeus and almost all military and political experts agree that there is no military solution in Afghanistan. In March 2009 President Obama announced an increase in US troops, saying he would decide on the strategy only *after* sending the troops. In June, he named General McChrystal as the new head of command in Afghanistan. With his background in special forces, McChrystal's job was to shift US military strategy from one of counterterrorism—killing bad guys like al-Qaeda before they try to attack us—to one of counterinsurgency, based on the strategy of "clear, hold, and build." (See page 121.)

Reconstruction and development are seen as the prime way to win the hearts and minds of the Afghan population, considered key to winning a counterinsurgency war. But so far the ratio of military to reconstruction spending is the polar opposite: 95+ percent to the military, and most of the reconstruction spending has gone to training, equipping, and arming the Afghan army and police.

Admiral Mullen testified on September 15, 2009, that "a properly resourced counter-insurgency probably means more forces, and without question, more time and more commitment to the protection of the Afghan people and to the development of good governance." Many estimate that it would take at least five to ten more years to achieve that goal.

By the time of Admiral Mullen's testimony, with US public opposition to the war above 50 percent and still growing, even the military was criticizing past Bush administration policies in Afghanistan. In perhaps one of the most candid, and scathing, condemnations of US military policies to date, one officer stated, "We haven't been fighting in Afghanistan for eight years. We've been fighting in Afghanistan for one year, eight years in a row."[154] But while acknowledging the failure of past military policies, many still argue for a military-based solution.

When 4,000 US Marines swept into southern Helmand province in July 2009, General Mc-Chrystal's stated goal was to protect the civilian population, not to kill terrorists or insurgents. Yet his counterinsurgency strategy identified protecting Afghans not as an end in itself but a means for the US to gain Afghan allies to fight for the primary US goal of protecting the *American* people by denying a safe haven to al-Qaeda. Part of the reason General McChrystal called for more troops is that the 4,000 troops originally sent to Helmand will need to stay there a long time if they are to ensure lasting security for the people. There seemed to be no strategy to protect communities in Khost and other provinces as insurgents shift their attacks to new venues. And ultimately, why would Afghan communities trust foreign troops willing to sacrifice Afghan lives to protect US lives they hold at a higher value?

One of the surest ways to escalate violence and endanger Afghan communities and civilians in any given area is to increase the foreign troop presence. The Taliban and other insurgents know they cannot take on large numbers of US forces in frontal attacks so they rely heavily on IEDs, bombings of government buildings and marketplaces, which invariably lead to greater civilian casualties—both from insurgent attacks and US strikes. The US military cannot expect to build trust with Afghan communities when the very presence of US troops increases instability.

The 1994 UN Human Development Report on "Human Security" documented that the higher the ratio of military to non-military government spending was in a country, the more unstable and the more vulnerable that country's people were to lack of health and education. Yet proponents and even some critics of US military escalation tend to advocate substantial investment in increasing the strength and capacity of Afghanistan's army and national police. The Afghan government has no capacity to pay for even 2009 security funding levels, let alone a major increase. Thus Afghanistan will be forced to be a foreign-dependent militia state for years to come, and large centralized army and police forces will drain away resources from critical infrastructure and civilian development needs.

As is true in many countries, Afghanistan's police force is plagued by corruption and extortion, making the police themselves one of the greatest sources of insecurity. Greater training by outsiders will not end corruption or enhance police account-ability to local communities. International funding would be better used for Afghan-led training of health workers and educators, and strengthening the Afghan judicial system to break the widening culture of impunity. Even General McChrystal noted that the Taliban's "establishment of ombudsmen to investigate abuse of power in its own cadres and remove those found guilty capitalizes on this [Kabul government's] weakness and attracts popular support for [the Taliban's] shadow government."[155]

Proponents of escalating US troop levels argue that this will strengthen the legitimate central government. But with widespread reports of election fraud, an ongoing US military presence will continue to be seen by Afghans as propping up a highly corrupt, discredited, and illegitimate administration.

While the US tries to buy local community support with military presence and big foreign-run reconstruction projects, the insurgents understand that many cups of tea with local shuras (community councils), combined with swift justice to root out corrupt local officials, will bring more respect and popular support.

Even George Will, the conservative commentator, has joined those who have proposed a "less is more" military solution: "forces should be substantially reduced," he said, "to serve a comprehensively revised policy."[156] And in March 2009, former head of the Council on Foreign Relations Leslie Gelb offered a "power extrication strategy" based on negotiating with the Taliban and making deals with a "coalition of neighbors" (Pakistan, India, Russia, Iran, China) to reduce tensions as US military forces gradually withdrew. For Gelb, the role of the US military should not be to "clear, hold, and build" but to "contain and deter."[157] Most Afghans, like most military analysts, know that al-Qaeda is no longer in Afghanistan but operates primarily out of Pakistan. If the military goal of the US was simply to remove al-Qaeda from Afghanistan, then why not declare success and leave?

What should US policy in Afghanistan look like?

The US war in Afghanistan isn't working—and isn't likely to work—to bring liberation, security, democracy, prosperity, or independence to Afghanistan. US policy needs to change, to move toward diplomacy and support for real development. That means the US needs to be prepared to accept styles of governance, an economy, and leaders that may not match its own preferences.

A US policy shift must start by ending the war in and occupation of Afghanistan, and ending the drone attacks on Pakistanis. The journalists Paul Fitzgerald and Elizabeth Gould, in their ground-breaking 2009 book *Invisible History: Afghanistan's Untold Story*, identify some of the steps the US should take in Afghanistan after almost a decade of lethal but failed war. Several of their proposed steps were obvious, others in the should-be-but-too-often-aren't-obvious category. They included:

· Stop killing Afghans
· Stop humiliating Afghan civilians and desecrating their homes
· Declare the "global war on terror" officially over
· Clarify US goals
· Listen to and take seriously the opinions of people knowledgeable in the diversity of Afghan political views
· Address the drug issue from the vantage point of the economic needs of poor farmers

The first goal is the most obvious and should be easiest. Even for those who do not believe that moral legitimacy should play a role in US foreign policy, there is an undisputed link between the killing of Afghan civilians and the widespread Afghan opposition to the role and very presence of the US in their country. Killing the people whose "hearts and minds" you are trying to win over is a pretty good guarantee of a losing strategy. In June 2009 the US and NATO commander in Afghanistan, General McChrystal, announced a change of strategy. From now on, he said, protecting Afghan civilians would be the top military priority, requiring troops to make what he called "a 'cultural shift' away from being a force designed for high-intensity combat."[158] But despite those words, the following four months saw civilian casualty levels among the highest of the war.

The dishonoring and desecration of Afghans and their homes, inherent in the attacks on houses, mosques, and other public spaces, has from the earliest days of the US war characterized what the US troop presence means for ordinary Afghans across the country. The lack of respect shown in those attacks has played a major role in building anti-US sentiment and indeed rising support for the insurgency. In his critique of the Pentagon's reliance on so-called strategic communications in place of real policy change, the chairman of the Joint Chiefs of Staff, Admiral Mike Mullen, acknowledged that "we need to worry a lot less about how to communicate our actions and much more about what our actions communicate. ... Only through a shared appreciation of the people's culture, needs and hopes for the future can we hope ourselves to supplant the extremist narrative."[159] But while the Obama administration has claimed a commitment to reducing the frequency of kick-in-the-door raids and other humiliating attacks on civilian targets, much of the new strategy appears to involve putting an Afghan face on the door-kicker rather than actually ending the tactic. The Israeli geographer Eyal Weisman, analyzing how the Israeli military uses the seizure and control of houses as a weapon of war, describes how the "unexpected penetration of war into the private domain of the home has been experienced by civilians in Palestine, just like in Iraq, as the most profound form of trauma and humiliation."[160] The same can be said of Afghans.

The Obama administration, just two months into office, officially made the "global war on terror" history. But only the phrase was ended, not the concept, and certainly not the cross-border reality. The March 2009 Pentagon memo read, "this administration prefers to avoid using the term 'Long War' or 'Global War on Terror' [GWOT]. Please use 'Overseas Contingency Operation.'"[161] But the shift in discourse did not reflect a shift in strategy. Whatever it was called, the US war continued—in Afghanistan, in Iraq, and apparently in the myriad covert and secret battles around the globe. In August 2009 the Obama administration announced its decision to maintain its elite counterinsurgency forces in the Philippines, where they had been deployed since 2002. Explaining the decision, the Pentagon spokesperson announced that what he called "international terrorist groups" in the Philippines "would ramp back up their attacks if we were to draw down" US troops.[162] In fact, those ostensible "international terrorists" were a violent but tiny gang of criminal thugs on one southern island who had been upgraded by the Bush administration's fiat in early 2002 to a new status as the just-discovered Southeast Asian branch of al-Qaeda. (It should be noted that the US commander of the force, claiming success, acknowledged that only 20 percent of his team's activities were military, the other 80 percent consisting of construction, health, development assistance— exactly the ratio Obama administration officials claim to want in Afghanistan, but a world away from the actual 98 percent military and 2 percent development spending.)

It is important to "clarify" US goals in Afghanistan in order to prevent mission creep. This would be the danger if, for example, a few years into President Obama's first or second terms, the government of a slightly more stable Afghanistan encourages the involvement and investment of US oil and gas companies to build pipelines across the country—and suddenly violence spikes again. Would additional US or NATO troops be sent, or would some of those already in Afghanistan be redeployed, to protect those US investments?

US policy should also be based on encouraging development in Afghanistan—a process that, in combination with a troop withdrawal, will also undermine support for the Taliban and other insurgent forces. That means investing in real development that benefits the people of Afghanistan, reversing the Iraq war practice of funding and relying on US-based corporate contractors, foreign suppliers, and mercenaries, "security experts," and others whose profits result in most of the aid funds remaining in the US, with only small proportions going directly to Afghans. As the *Economist* described it, "to most Afghan eyes, watching heavily guarded foreign aid-workers glide by in their Landcruisers, it is obvious that much of the money is going straight back out of the country."[163]

The assessment of Carnegie scholar Gilles Dorronsoro should not be forgotten: "the presence of foreign troops is the most important element driving the resurgence of the Taliban."[164] This would include anthropologists or aid workers dressed, armed, and embedded with those foreign troops.

What diplomatic options does the US have?

The Obama administration needs to replace its military campaigns with diplomacy in and around Afghanistan. Direct engagement with the Taliban may be politically difficult at home. But it must be sought in the context of a much wider diplomatic effort that brings to the table not only the powerful ethnic and tribal militia leaders the US has long sponsored (many of whom are as repressive and misogynistic as the Taliban), but also representatives of Afghanistan's broad and diverse civil society. That means ensuring a voice for local and provincial as well as national leaders, both rural and urban, women and men, religious and secular, who actually have far more influence on the lives of Afghan people than any of the US-backed government officials.

That diplomacy will have to include a regional component as well. As Fitzgerald and Gould describe it,

> Today's dilemma for the Afghans, be they anti-extremist Pashtuns, Tajiks, Hazaras or Uzbeks, is rooted deeply in the history of czarist, Napoleonic, Kaiserian, Nazi, British, Soviet, Chinese, Iranian, American and Pakistani efforts to use Afghanistan for their own grand designs. Any solution that does not recognize the need for those nations to counter the legacy of foreign-supported extremism with an extended commitment to civil society and nation building, cannot hope to formulate a successful policy.[165]

The US should recognize that it has no greater right than any other nation to call the shots in a regional or international diplomatic process that must ultimately be led by Afghans themselves.

Certainly regional and global diplomatic efforts aimed at actually ending the war face enormous challenges. Even aside from the Obama administration's stated commitment to continuing the war until some version of "success," other outside actors are in no hurry to end the war. Russia's 2009 shift, allowing NATO to transit Russian territory en route to Afghanistan, was based on the assumption that the US/NATO war in Afghanistan would continue for years. Moscow responded with its campaign to rebuild relations with US and NATO in the post-Bush era. At the same time, Russia offered acquiescence to the Afghan war as a carrot, hoping to dissuade NATO from offering membership to Ukraine and Georgia.

Pakistan provides an even greater regional challenge, with much of its military leadership, especially the ISI, its powerful intelligence agency, eager to maintain the Taliban as a bulwark against perceived Indian, as well as US, NATO, Iranian, and Russian influence in Afghanistan. Diplomatic engagement with Pakistan will have to include an end to US drone attacks and ending the US habit of arming, paying, and allying itself with the Pakistani military. That habit further weakens the already feeble (as well as undemocratic and corrupt) civilian government. As in Afghanistan, the US will have to shift from a military alliance with Pakistan to a diplomatic posture that recognizes Pakistan's sophisticated and experienced network of civil society mobilization, which has survived despite decades of militarism and repression.

Once the US military campaign actually begins to wind down, diplomacy will not be as difficult. There have already been calls for a regional summit including all of Afghanistan's neighbors as well as the UN, the Organization of the Islamic Conference, and the powerful actors involved in the war. While virtually every NATO government other than the US and Britain has complied with their publics' demands for reduction or full

ENDING THE US WAR IN AFGHANISTAN

withdrawal of troops from Afghanistan, people and governments alike appear more and more eager to engage in real development and reconstruction assistance.

In the longer term, US "Afghanistan policy" will need to include the transformation of broader policy toward the Middle East and Central Asia. This would mean ending US support for undemocratic, dictatorial regimes that continue their violations of international law and human rights across those strategic regions. Throughout these lands, US economic, military, and political support is blamed for bolstering, arming, and/or financing Israel's occupation of Palestinian land; Egypt's repressive family dynasty posing as a democracy; Saudi Arabia's corruption and oppression of women; the absolute monarchies of the tiny Gulf petro-states that deny all rights to non-citizen majorities in their countries; Uzbekistan's horrifying reliance on torture; as well as for keeping in power corrupt governments of questionable legitimacy in Iraq and Afghanistan. And indeed, that popular understanding of US accountability is largely correct. In return for these policies, the US gets reliable allies, access to and control of oil and gas, and military bases from those governments—but faces anger, opposition, some-times hatred from their people. Only a tiny fraction of people, like al-Qaeda, imagine doing harm to the US or to Americans in return—but if these unpopular and dangerous policies were changed, it would be nearly impossible for those isolated terrorists plotting attacks on civilians to find the support they needed to carry them out.

As Chairman of the Joint Chiefs of Staff Admiral Mullen has said, "strategic communication problems are not communication problems at all. They are policy and execution problems. Each time we fail to live up to our values or don't follow up on a promise, we look more and more like the arrogant Americans the enemy claims we are."[166] When decades of US policy—backing torture, illegal occupations, absolute monarchs, and brutal dictatorships—fly in the face of claimed US support for self-determination and democracy, everyone in the United States is made less safe.

What would happen if the US ended air strikes and pulled all the troops out of Afghanistan?

No one can be certain what will happen when US and NATO troops are pulled out of Afghanistan, when US air strikes end, when US covert counterinsurgency operations are halted. Some of the most respected outside Afghanistan experts, however, are very clear that the revitalization of the Taliban's armed insurgency that took shape in 2008 and beyond would be reversed. Gilles Dorronsoro of the Carnegie Endowment, for instance, as quoted above, recognized that "the presence of foreign troops is the most important element driving the resurgence of the Taliban." Without those troops, the Taliban's renewal would slow, and then perhaps stall and finally be reversed.

The most important result of the US/NATO withdrawal—whenever it takes place—will be its impact on the people of Afghanistan. The troop withdrawal and end of air strikes will not, unfortunately, result in an immediate peace; the consequences of years of US and other international meddling and wars fought in and over Afghanistan will continue to take a devastating toll on the Afghan people for decades to come. Afghanistan does not have a long history of strong central governments, and local, regional, tribal, and other power centers, including militia leaders all-too-well-armed with the detritus of earlier wars, will likely continue fighting for larger shares of wealth, power, land, and influence.

So reducing, even ending, the violence committed by occupation forces and resistance to occupation forces will not lead immediately to the complete demilitarization and de-weaponization of Afghan society. But the end of occupation and the end of air strikes carried out by occupation forces, causing far too frequent civilian deaths, will reduce violence. An example might be that of Basra, an oil-rich city in southern Iraq. Basra had been occupied by British troops from the earliest days of the US–

UK invasion in 2003. When the British troops pulled back from the city center in 2007, military attacks dropped by 90 percent. The British general in command said, "we thought, if 90 percent of the violence is directed at us, what would happen if we stepped back?" Analyzing the impact of those 5,000 British troops moving out of the heart of Basra, he described "a remarkable and dramatic drop in attacks. The motivation for attacking us was gone, because we're no longer patrolling the streets." British officials said they expected a spike in what they called "intra-militia violence" after their troops pulled back, but were surprised to find none.[167]

What the end of the US/NATO military involvement will allow, for the first time, is a far greater effort than that currently underway to make good on the huge debt the US owes the people of Afghanistan. Far from "abandoning" the people of that war-torn country, a military withdrawal is the necessary first step toward a serious campaign of financial, development, humanitarian, environmental, and other kinds of reparations and reconstruction. As long as 90 percent or more of US funding for Afghanistan goes to continuing a war despite its descent into a quagmire, there will be no funds, and little political support, for providing billions of dollars in real reconstruction. Neither the people of Afghanistan, nor its neighbors, nor US allies, nor the UN or the international community as a whole will take seriously US efforts to help heal Afghanistan as long as it continues to occupy the country and kill civilians there. Such confidence can only begin to be built once the US war in Afghanistan is winding down, and troops are moving out, rather than new brigades moving in.

It is certainly possible that the Kabul government installed and kept in power by US/NATO military backing might not survive a withdrawal of foreign troops. That stark situation, similar to the situation in US-occupied Iraq, reflects the reality that the government led by President Hamid Karzai, elected or not, has probably not created enough domestic legitimacy and credibility among the Afghan people to survive on its own as a truly independent, sovereign government relying for support on the willing consent of the governed.

What political forces would emerge to fill a post-occupation partial or total vacuum remains uncertain; what role the Taliban will play is likely to reflect what kind of negotiations or diplomatic engagement goes on during the process of military withdrawal. A political power struggle is certain. The degree to which that power struggle can take a primarily nonviolent and political, rather than military, character depends a great deal on whether Afghanistan's ravaged civil society, secular as well as religious, will have survived years of war and

occupation with enough strength to challenge the
military force of the wide range of Mujahideen and
other armed opposition groups.

So is the war in Afghanistan actually necessary
to stop al-Qaeda? In 2009, the influential analytical
website Stratfor described the divergence between
the war in Afghanistan and Washington's claimed
strategic interests regarding al-Qaeda:

> It is not clear that al Qaeda prime [the central
> group based around Osama bin Laden] is
> operational anymore. Some members remain,
> putting out videos now and then and trying to
> appear fearsome, but it would seem that US
> operations have crippled al Qaeda.... So if the
> primary reason for fighting the Taliban is to keep
> al Qaeda prime from having a base of operations
> in Afghanistan, that reason might be moot now as
> al Qaeda appears to be wrecked.... It is there-
> fore no longer clear that resisting the Taliban is
> essential for blocking al Qaeda: al Qaeda may
> simply no longer be there. (At this point, the
> burden of proof is on those who think al Qaeda
> remains operational.)[168]

So far, that burden of proof has not been met.

Certainly no one can absolutely guarantee what
will happen when US and NATO troops leave
Afghanistan. But it is clear what will happen if they
remain: more of the deadly spiral of violence that
continues to claim the lives of Afghan civilians and
US troops. Withdrawal is the first step toward

allowing the people of Afghanistan to reclaim, rebuild, and recreate their country.

If so many people oppose the war, why is it so hard to change the Obama administration's policy and end it?

President Obama has been consistent from the moment of his inauguration and even before that he intended to continue and to escalate the US war in Afghanistan. Despite clear majority US public opposition, despite the decision by the virtually every NATO government with troops in Afghanistan to withdraw or downsize or constrain the mandate of their soldiers, despite recognition by Obama and his military leaders that there is no solely military solution in Afghanistan—despite it all, the only part of US strategy in Afghanistan that is expanding is the military part. More US troops, more attack helicopters, more drone bombers, more war funding—more war.

The political discourse on the war has changed, and will change further. By August 2009 most people in the US did not believe the US can win the war and did not believe it should continue. Fifty-four percent said they oppose the war. Afghanistan is no longer viewed as the "good war." There is no question that the antiwar movement has played a key role in those shifts. But the education, advocacy, and active mobilization needed to transform the change in discourse into a change of policy have all stalled. Challenging what is widely described as "Obama's war" has proved difficult.

Part of the reason lies in the nature of the antiwar movement that cohered to challenge George W. Bush's "global war on terror." From the beginning, that movement was as much anti-Bush as it was antiwar. Bush's actions—far beyond the wars themselves and the slashing of domestic civil liberties that accompanied the global wars—created movements against his policies on the environment, economic justice and privatization, racism, women's rights, healthcare, labor rights, and much more. The antiwar movement emerged as the vanguard of challenges to the whole spectrum of US policies of endless war and privileging the rich, which reflected an awareness across social movements that all their specific concerns faced the terrible consequences of Bush's wars in Afghanistan and Iraq. From the beginning, the antiwar movement shared an almost visceral opposition to George W. Bush and his administration.

The inauguration of President Obama transformed the overall political environment, despite the fact that changes in the strategic/ military arena were too slow and too few. Obama as a person and as a candidate was hailed as the "anti-Bush," or at least "not Bush." And so his administration's policies were assumed to also be the opposite of Bush's. On some domestic issues in the first months of the administration that was relatively accurate, but on issues of war and militarism, there was far more continuity with the past. The Iraq war continued; although the war changed somewhat as US combat troops drew back from cities, 130,000 US troops remained deployed in the country. The Afghanistan war escalated; intervention in Pakistan was on the rise, and casualties rose in both. The danger of US escalation against Iran continued, although the militarist rhetoric was less bellicose than in the past.

For the public, however, the world appeared very different. Even with widespread discussion of the challenges and failures of "Obama's war," opposing the war no longer necessarily means opposing the president. For the majority of the people who do indeed want to end the wars, the White House is not only *not* the enemy or even the main opponent, it is often—perhaps too often— viewed as a potential antiwar ally.

Obama was inaugurated president in the midst of the worst financial crisis since the 1930s. That meant that initially his wars—Iraq, Afghanistan, Pakistan, Iran—no longer claimed the pride of place in public attention, despite their central role in causing the economic disaster. By the spring and summer of 2009, however, as US as well as civilian casualties in Afghanistan mounted, headlines and public attention returned at least partly to the urgency of the wars. But circumstances had changed, and organizing remained difficult.

For some people the problem was war fatigue—a combination of frustration born of years of the Bush administration ignoring antiwar majorities, exhaustion with the seeming endless-ness of the wars, and a hope, disguised as belief, that Obama's antiwar stance regarding Iraq would somehow be extended to Afghanistan. For others the obstacle was Obama himself—the election of the first African-American president represented the culmination of so many years of struggle and sacrifice that many were unwilling to acknowledge an end to the triumph and hope of that powerful victory over racism by beginning to criticize the president's policies. Still others continued to point to the extraordinary breadth of the grassroots mobilization that, for the first time since FDR's second term more than 70 years earlier, elected a US president *because of* his antiwar stance. They believed—or at least wanted to believe—that the existence of such a movement somehow guaranteed White House accountability to it.

Individually, each of these views made sense. But taken together, all of them also contributed to the antiwar movements' diminished power and lack of strategic clarity.

Antiwar activists watched as the Obama

administration, at least in its early months, showed itself significantly more willing than any of its recent predecessors to include progressive voices in policy debates, primarily on domestic issues. (That openness diminished during the spring 2009 healthcare debate, when supporters of the widely popular single-payer system were explicitly banished from the discussion.) Of course access did not guarantee influence, but for a while it appeared that progressive and grassroots-based voices would not be marginalized, at least on the issues in which administration policies were in the same ballpark as key supporters had urged. That provided new opportunities for progressives in the labor, economic justice, and parts of the environmental movements. But strong challengers to Obama's left were rarely welcomed as legitimate participants in the official policy debates in arenas such as war and peace, where from the beginning Obama admini-stration policies diverged profoundly from the views of a wide majority of his supporters.

In response, one approach claimed the Obama White House *was* no different than the Bush administration, and that the job of the peace movement should be to convince people that Obama should be treated as a war criminal just like Bush. That approach was dramatically wrong. Real significant policy differences remain, even though the wars have continued. Antiwar advocacy has always aimed at winning people to an antiwar position—when we address an antiwar constituency that already believes Obama is its ally, we should build on that strength, not try to reverse what people feel so strongly. And while the overall US system of seeking empire has not ended, the specific ideological foundation of the Bush presidency—based on a reckless unilateralism and militarism—is no longer operative.

An Obama presidency presents new and different challenges for those mobilizing against the wars in Iraq and Afghanistan. Certainly there must be clear, unequivocal, and uncompromising opposition to Obama's escalation in Afghanistan and Pakistan, his continuation of the Iraq war, as well as his continuing threats (albeit quieter) against Iran and support for the Israeli occupation. The question is *how* to engage and mobilize the huge numbers of people who see President Obama as a symbol of their own years of struggle, who worked harder than they had ever worked before to put him in the White House, who are prepared to cut President Obama all kinds of slack—but who still want a real end to the wars, and are dissatisfied, even furious, with Obama's policies. *How* do we mobilize in a way that recognizes, even while challenging, some people's view that voting for Obama was a sufficient antiwar action? How do we reach the three or four million people, especially young people, who actively campaigned for Obama, and recruit them to further activism as a central core of a new antiwar movement? And how do we claim to represent them—even while we are urging them to challenge the symbol of their mobilization? How does the antiwar movement build on its powerful position within the broad election mobilization, which was based on the primacy of Obama's own opposition to war in his campaign?

What would a responsible plan to end the US war in Afghanistan look like?

When President Obama claimed the war in Afghanistan as his own, he did not have a plan for an end game. The goals and definition of "victory" of the US war in Afghanistan changed during the first months of his presidency. According to the *Economist*, "as the West struggles to maintain its weak hold on Afghanistan, so its ambitions there are narrowing. Early aspirations to bring peace, prosperity and decent government to the country have been replaced by the hope of establishing a functioning state and of improved security. By that measure, success in the short term will look much like stalemate."[169]

And by any measure, by the end of summer 2009, with a clear majority of Americans opposed to the war in Afghanistan, members of Congress and the public were still demanding an exit strategy from an administration that didn't have one. As was true in Iraq, there was much talk of the dangers of ending the war in Afghanistan.

But with all the discussion of the dangers of withdrawal, there is little acknowledgement of the dangers if the war continues. It may not be surprising that editors of the *Economist* don't prioritize concerns about Afghan civilian deaths or even escalating numbers of US and NATO troop casualties. But one might wonder how they managed to forgot to mention the danger so many experts have recognized, that the presence of US and NATO troops is precisely what fuels the insurgency in the first place.

As was the case with Iraq, many people, including those committed to ending the war, are concerned that the US not simply "cut and run" from Afghanistan. That phrase was memorably claimed by the Iraq war's supporters to discredit and undermine the war's opponents; those who used the term in fact cared little about Iraqi civilians, of whom more than a million had already died as a result of the war. But it *was* true in Iraq and is equally true in Afghanistan that the US debt to the people of those beleaguered countries is far greater than just getting the troops out. After years of war, abandonment to brutal US-armed warlords, invasion, occupation, more war—the US owes a huge debt to the Afghan people. Pulling out the troops is only step one.

Certainly the exact means of executing a rapid withdrawal of troops from Afghanistan, as in Iraq, is a tactical move that Pentagon logisticians will have to plan—using the same combinations of trucks, planes, helicopters, and perhaps donkeys that they used to invade and occupy Afghanistan in the first place. But beyond the withdrawal of troops, what would a responsible plan to end the war in Afghanistan require?

· Recognize what the war in Afghanistan is doing (killing civilians, building antagonism toward the US, building support for insurgents) and what it is incapable of doing (occupying forces can't end local support for insurgency when insurgency is defined as "anti-occupation"; military can't successfully do development work).

· Immediately end troop escalation and all combat and counterinsurgency operations in Afghanistan; immediately halt drone attacks and threatened escalation in Pakistan; close all US military bases in Afghanistan; begin full withdrawal of all US troops from Afghanistan.

· Stop identifying humanitarian aid workers as "force multipliers" and remove all humanitarian, development, infrastructure, or other assistance programs and personnel from control of the military.

· Immediately close Bagram Airbase prison; help current Afghan government (as long as it remains in power) as well as local and provincial authorities expand social programs available for former detainees (including a substantial cash infusion for job training and jobs).

· Immediately increase refugee assistance: financial assistance for returning refugees to Afghanistan and assistance to main refugee centers (Iran, Pakistan); accept more refugees into US.

· Stop all anti-poppy fumigation programs; invest significant funds in infrastructure and financial assistance for alternative crop cultivation.

· Promote and support (but do not control/dominate) ceasefire, reconciliation, and negotiation processes involving all parties including Taliban in both Afghanistan and Pakistan; encourage major roles for local and regional leaders, ethnic-based and nationalist, religious and secular, rural and urban, including women and community-based and civil society representation. Support real, not simply titular, control by the UN, Afghan civil society groups, and others; do not impose US choices for leaders.

· Recognize the scale of corruption and illegitimacy in the US-backed government; end uncritical political and financial backing.

· Provide financial assistance distributed in small-scale amounts to local, regional, tribal, and other leaders for job creation, aiming particularly at reaching and recruiting young unemployed men

who are vulnerable to militias offering pay
(insurgent or pro-government).

· Support but do not control separate negotiations
including all neighboring countries, with leadership
of UN, the Organization of the Islamic Conference
(OIC), the Shanghai Cooperation Alliance (which
groups China, Russia, and five resource-rich
Central Asian states), other regional organizations;
negotiations should include all political actors but
exclude NATO, CSTO, and other military alliances.

· Immediately begin shifting the majority of
Afghanistan military budgets into UN and regional
funds for Afghan-chosen, Afghan-planned, and
Afghan-implemented construction and reconstruction. Use the remaining budget to fund US
troop withdrawal. Initiate funding relations with
UN agencies, other international development
organizations, and governments to create Afghan-
controlled capacity-building and training institutions, with at least 90 percent of allocated funds
going directly into Afghan (not US or other
international corporate or contractor) hands.

What policy choices would prevent future Afghanistan-style quagmires?

· Shift all budgets for international, including
Afghan, development, education, health, water,
infrastructure, governance, and police out of the
Pentagon and into the State Department; consider

creation of a new international development department with an independent cabinet seat, in order to create and implement a development strategy based on the interests of poorest countries and peoples, not based on either US military (Pentagon) or traditionally defined US national (State Department) interests.

· Redirect part of the war budget to carry out research and create jobs in producing alternative fuels and energy sources, aimed at reducing US dependence on *all* oil, not only imported oil.

· Support negotiations for a Nuclear Weapons–Free Zone in the Middle East, and for broadening the existing Central Asian NWFZ to include Afghanistan.

· Close all US military bases in the Middle East and Central Asia.

· Initiate a broad-stroke reevaluation of overall US policy in the Middle East and Central Asia, including a new definition of "national interest" away from traditional triplet of oil, Israel, and stability.

What will it take to change US policy in Afghanistan?

The end of eight years of George Bush's unilateralism and militarism and the inauguration of Barack Obama has ushered in a new political period. The US war in Afghanistan has actually gotten worse, with civilian deaths rising and US and

NATO military casualties escalating as well, but this is not the same war. It cannot be opposed the same way. We will need innovative ways of building and shaping a new kind of movement—which means not only new tactics to reflect the new period, but new strategic alliances between those focusing specifically on changing US policy and ending the US war in Afghanistan and those engaged in responding to the economic crisis.

The work of challenging the costs of illegal and failing wars, and demanding that the military budget be slashed to free up urgently needed funds for green jobs, education, health, and infrastructure repair all remain more crucial than ever. A focus on the costs of war empowers the broader mobilization that is working to respond to the needs of people caught in the economic crisis, as well as strengthening new and stronger alliances with a wider range of people and organizations challenging not only the war profiteers but the overall economic crisis and those who created it.

Into the Streets

The work of showing—of demonstrating—the size and power of antiwar opinion across the country remains crucial. Street protests remain vitally important. But a street protest, a march, a rally can also "demonstrate" weakness instead of strength, so it's necessary always to gauge when the time is right for public actions. National and nationally coordinated regional and local protests and demonstrations will need to continue; often events held simultaneously in many diverse locations will result in more powerful impact than national marches and rallies that may involve far fewer participants than during the height of anti-Bush mobilization. Those street protests can be strengthened by linking to petition drives and campaigns aimed at reaching local/municipal/state officials, and built on by following them with teach-ins, lobby days, and other related actions.

Ironically, the severity of the economic crisis, the threat of global warming, many of the legacies of the Bush years' attacks on civil liberties, mean that those mobilized against war in Afghanistan will likely represent a broad range of communities affected by the war in numerous ways—as well as key existing constituencies such as veterans, young people, Arabs and other people of color, Muslims, and many more.

Congress

Congress is an institution grounded in compromise. Despite courageous stands taken by some individual members, Congress will never lead the difficult campaigns such as ending funding for a failing war—but its members will, when and if political pressure rises high enough, follow the lead of public opinion.

Recognizing this new political period also means taking into account that Democrats, even (perhaps especially) progressive Democrats, remain reluctant to openly challenge President Obama. Those who are willing tend to do so relatively quietly. Continuing public pressure on Congress will therefore be necessary as long as the war continues.

The politically driven fear—not fear of what might actually happen to the troops but fear of being *accused* of abandoning the troops—that leads to Congress's refusal to stop funding the war, is certainly an ongoing problem. But the moment Congress perceives that the political cost of funding the war has risen above the cost of *ending* the war, they will do what has become politically expedient—and cutting war funding will become an urgent political necessity. The pressure will take many forms, and will involve combined "inside/outside" strategies—from phone-in and lobby days and letter-writing drives, to constituent demands that members of Congress participate in open discussions and town hall meetings and debates on the costs of war, to working with congressional and committee staff on potential legislation and "dear colleague" letters, to mobilizing protests inside or outside members' headquarters in their home districts or in their Capitol offices in Washington, DC.

Education

Building a powerful movement against the US war in Afghanistan means providing people with the tools they need to argue the case to those who don't already agree. It doesn't mean everyone must become an overnight expert on the history of US intervention in Afghanistan, but everyone needs to learn the basics. Afghanistan—as a place with real people, culture, history—is even less known than Iraq to people in the US. So education must retain the pride of place for all those trying to end the war. Strong convictions and moral outrage alone will never be enough to convince those who disagree, or persuade those in power to act on antiwar opinions. Opponents of the war need strong arguments and irrefutable facts to move beyond their comfort zones and reach out to broader audiences. Clear and concise information is needed to counter those who argue "but Afghanistan is the good war," or "we can't just cut and run," or "we have to stay because there will be chaos if we leave" or "we have to fight them there so we don't have to fight them here" or "we have to win the war because they hate us." New resources, using books and pamphlets, television and radio shows, online and interactive discussions, websites and social networking, new media tools and much more must all be utilized. Teach-ins, classes, and discussions at high schools and universities, publication in mainstream and progressive media outlets, book groups and discussions, claiming public spaces such as libraries for new kinds of interactive events—all must be part of the antiwar arsenal.

Costs of War

Mobilizing against an unjust, illegal, and immoral war in the midst of the worst economic crisis in two generations is both easier and more difficult. It is more difficult because people struggling with job loss, house foreclosure, lack of healthcare, rising college tuition, and so much more, have little time or energy to focus on broader international issues that so often seem disconnected from day-to-day crises. On the other hand, it is easier because people who are hurting directly, when presented with clear and accessible information, are more open to hearing and interacting with new ideas about why the economy has collapsed (hundreds of billions spent on the military) and where money might be found to support critically needed social spending (hundreds of billions shifted from the war budgets).

This will be particularly important in the context of troop escalations. Every 1,000 US soldiers will cost $1 billion per year. So General McChrystal's call for 40,000 or more new troops would cost more than $40 billion every year—on top of the existing hundreds of billions of war costs.

Organizations like the National Priorities Project continue to play a hugely important role in providing the antiwar movement with concrete factual information showing the direct links between the costs of war and the social programs left undone at home. They break down the seemingly mind-numbing numbers of the federal budget into comparisons—in each town, or each congressional district, or each state—how much for education, how much for healthcare, vs. how much for war.

The focus on costs—always keeping in mind that costs include human, environmental, human rights, international law, and other costs as well as financial—means that building a movement against the war in Afghanistan will require new and stronger and more strategic relationships with other organizations and coalitions and movements, many of them grounded in communities of color, that are growing in direct response to the economic crisis and fighting for justice-based, rather than the Wall Street bailout–style, solutions to it.

Afghan Victims, Afghan Voices

Far too often the opinions of the people whose lives are most affected by the war—Afghan civilians—are ignored. This is not because those opinions are unknown. A February 2009 poll across Afghanistan, carried out by a consortium of ABC News, the

BBC, and ARD German TV, showed that the number of Afghans who say their country is headed in the right direction had dropped to 40 percent, from a high of 77 percent back in 2005. During the same period, Afghans expressing a favorable overall view of the United States dropped from 83 percent to less than half—down to 47 percent in 2009.[170] Certainly polls have their limitations, including the difficulty for pollsters in Afghanistan in conducting an accurate tally across a large and diverse country where so many people live in isolated villages. But the numbers do show a powerful shift.

It is also difficult to find Afghans outside their country who are prepared to publicly criticize the war—for all of the obvious reasons, starting with justifiable fear for themselves and their families back home. But there are some Afghans who have made the decision to speak publicly, people like the young Afghan parliamentarian Malalai Joya, who was expelled from the parliament and survived assassination attempts because of her criticism of both the US/NATO occupation of her country and the ruthlessness of the warlords in and outside of the government, and who spends much of her time speaking around the world. Those people should be featured voices in the US, as part of the effort to keep discussion of the costs of war focused on those who pay the biggest price. Delegations of women, labor, and families of 9/11 victims have all traveled to Afghanistan to meet their counterparts and to bring back Afghan voices.

Divisions at the Top

By the time Afghanistan became "Obama's war," popular support for the war had dwindled. By the end of summer 2009, with Afghanistan in the throes of strategic and tactical flip-flops and reversals, opposition was rising not only from the public but from a host of unexpected powerful media, official, and military voices. Suddenly there was no elite consensus on the war in Afghanistan, a reality that makes antiwar mobilization simultaneously more complicated and potentially more powerful.

With his troop escalation well underway, President Obama was increasingly finding congressional support only from the conservative wing of his own party, and from an enthusiastic majority of Republicans. The Congressional Progressive Caucus, even its more courageous individual members, were cautious in their opposition, but it became clear that Afghanistan was no longer the "good war" in Congress either. And as the rapid strategic shifts continued to fail, they brought new fears of defeat, quagmire, and an LBJ-in-Vietnam-style guns-or-butter fear of losing Obama's domestic priorities. That led to the emergence of a whole new range of conservative voices. Right-wing standard-bearer George Will led the pack, asking "why are we still in Afghanistan?" and concluding that genius "sometimes consists of knowing when to stop."[171] Conservative historian and retired colonel Andrew Bacevich recognized that new presidents don't get a "do-over"[172] and that Obama can't restart war in Afghanistan. And by mid-November 2009 even the US ambassador to Afghanistan, Karl W. Eikenberry, a retired general who once commanded US forces there, expressed "reservations" about deploying any additional US troops, even as President Obama weighed the size of the anticipated escalation.[173]

Such broad opposition can help build and legitimize antiwar opinions, but it requires serious efforts to figure out new ways of engaging with power. Recognizing and dealing with strange bedfellows must not mean accepting their power-driven, US-centric vantage point, or their generally limited critique of the war. But when George Will—as Henry Kissinger and Brent Scowcroft and James Baker and others did with Iraq—stakes out a position opposing military recklessness and urging caution, that's important. Those opinions matter a great deal, and should be used to strengthen the peace movement's own influence and legitimacy. Opponents of the war in Afghanistan should recognize that the elites' willingness to challenge Obama's war publicly rather than in secret has everything to do with the political protection provided by rising public opposition to the war. And that opposition is itself rooted in the earlier Iraq-focused antiwar movement's success in transforming public opinion, so that asserting an antiwar position no longer carries political risk.

Inside / Outside

Engaging with power always requires a complex web combining inside and outside strategies. Some of those working to end the war need to be inside, in the room, working with members of Congress or trying to engage directly with Obama administration officials who might be trying to reduce slightly the damage done by one particular war policy. Perhaps it is a bill to cut off spending for drone attacks in Pakistan or to demand an immediate closure of the prison at Bagram Airbase. None of those incremental changes will end the war. But they can sometimes mitigate some of the most egregious suffering; they can sometimes provide a much-needed victory, however short-term, for rising antiwar voices in Congress; sometimes they can serve as the first step on what one hopes will be a slippery slope to ending the war.

Others, by far the majority of grassroots war opponents and peace activists, will remain outside the room, and will defend the movement's principle of demanding a *real* end to the war.

There is an inherent tension between inside and outside strategies. That tension is even greater under the Obama administration, where there is much more access to administration officials on some issues (much more frequently on labor, some environmental, or trade than on war and peace questions) than during the Bush era, and in some arenas antiwar and progressive allies are actually in positions of authority (if not always real power) in the administration. That can blur the inside/outside distinction, and great care will be needed to avoid confusion and cooptation.

Those working inside need always to remember that what is "possible" in Congress or the White House—even in the Obama administration—will never be all of what is needed. Those working inside need the voices outside that continue to demand real peace, real justice, even as they themselves slog through tiny steps that seem so far from the goal. President Obama has not yet repeated the words of FDR, who famously told his progressive supporters pushing him on New Deal policies, "go out there and make me do it." But those working the inside tracks in the Obama administration will have to make that call.

Those working outside need to see that the danger is not in the achievement of the too-small and limited victories. The danger lies in abandoning principles and settling for "the possible" instead of continuing to fight for what is truly necessary: ending the war. Which must include making good on US obligations to the people of Afghanistan for reconstruction, development, real humanitarian assistance. The danger is not in winning small steps toward those goals; the danger is the antiwar movement giving in and accepting those limited "inside" victories as the ultimate goal.

Within the intersecting inside and outside strategies, different organizations and coalitions will often play different but collaborative roles. Sometimes individuals from the same organizations or institutions will take separate responsibilities for working inside and outside. And once in a while individuals will move from off-the-record congressional staff or administration meetings where efforts are underway to limit one or another specific aspects of the war, to leading street protests outside where the focus remains on *ending* the war, not simply reducing its harm.

Alternative Centers of Power

With the end of the Bush administration and a Democratic Congress elected alongside the Obama White House, one might have hoped for a much more empowered Congress prepared to push the president further toward the positions of those who elected them. But that has not been the case. That means that antiwar forces must continue to broaden our definitions of where influence lies, expanding what it means to engage with power.

The Cities for Peace movement, which began at the Institute for Policy Studies in the fall of 2002 many months before the invasion of Iraq, provides one such example. The movement organized in cities, counties, and states, focusing on mobilizing support for city council resolutions or mayors' proclamations opposing the war and demanding that US troops be brought home. Many of the resolutions focused on the illegality of the war, some honed in on why local National Guard or reserve troops should be brought home, almost all expressed outrage at how local resources—financial, human, first-responder capacity and more—were being squandered on an illegal and/or unnecessary and/or failing war. Similar campaigns are now underway focusing on the US war in Afghanistan.

Campaigns that organize around the costs of war at the local, congressional district, or state level have two major strengths. First, engaging with citizens at the local level encourages more people to engage directly in civic activism than is often the case in campaigns to challenge national policies. Second, they provide an immediate link to the costs of war at a scale and in language that everyone can understand. Three trillion dollars, the overall cost for the Iraq war, is impossible to grasp. But everyone can grasp the reality that their own town is paying X amount of tax money for the war, and that those same funds *could* have been used to provide health insurance for X number of children, or to build X number of low-cost housing units, or to hire X number of new teachers for impoverished schools in their own town.

Weakening the War Machine

As has been true throughout the Iraq war, growing resistance within the military has emerged as a key component of antiwar organizing, even beyond the rising public recognition of the war in Afghanistan's escalating human and economic costs. Counter-recruitment campaigns continue to play a crucial role in depriving the military of the man- and woman-power needed to actually wage war. The National Priorities Project, beyond their work on the war budget, was the first organization to document the class basis of military recruiting— tracking the income levels, town populations, and other factors showing which high schools are prioritized and which are bypassed by military recruiters. Iraq Veterans Against the War, which from its origins also included veterans returning from Afghanistan, have shaped their own "truth in recruiting" campaign.

Beyond the anti-recruitment drives, resistance *within* the armed services has emerged as a major center of antiwar attention and as a major concern for the Pentagon. The "Winter Soldier—Iraq and Afghanistan" hearing sponsored by Iraq Veterans Against the War in February 2008, and repeated on Capitol Hill in May, brought the reality of the Iraq and Afghanistan wars to hundreds of thousands, perhaps millions of people who watched the live web-cast, listened to radio coverage, read the transcripts, or saw clips on television. The hearings documented, through searing testimony by the veterans themselves, how public claims about "protecting civilians" were ignored in the theater of war. That history raises serious questions about how—indeed *whether*—similar orders at the heart of the 2009 "new strategy" for counterinsurgency in Afghanistan will be obeyed.

Choosing Sides

The broad US, NATO member countries', and global movements against the war and occupation in Afghanistan encompass a diverse range of organizations, coalitions, and campaigns. Traditional peace and antiwar organizations are partnering with campaigners for economic justice in the face of the international financial crisis. Mobilizations bringing together women's organizations, African-American community groups, movements fighting for living wage laws, gay and lesbian groups, global justice movements, and many more, all find themselves facing the Afghanistan war as a key target.

And, at the end of the day, our movements will only be as strong as our partnerships with our counterparts and colleagues around the world. The US government remains the key perpetrator of the war in Afghanistan, but other governments are there too, eager to back Washington's war. The US antiwar movement has a special role to play, but we cannot do it alone. Internationalism—meaning building our ties with and helping promote the voice of Afghan war opponents, strengthening our alliances with the global peace movement, claiming the United Nations as our own—must remain the centerpiece of all our work.

NOTES

1 Tyler Marshall and Paul Watson, "Afghans Teeter on Edge," *Los Angeles Times* 17 Sept. 2001 <articles.latimes.com/2001/sep/17/ news/mn-46646>

2 Chris Matthews, "Who Hijacked Our War?" *San Francisco Chronicle* 17 Feb. 2002.

3 Michael Kinsley, "What Is Terrorism, Continued," *Slate* 7 Feb. 2002 <www.slate.com/id/2061783/>

4 Tyler Marshall and Paul Watson, "Afghans Teeter on Edge," *Los Angeles Times* 17 Sept. 2001.

5 Dave Cook, "Obama's Trip to Canada Will Highlight Differences on Afghanistan," *Christian Science Monitor* 17 Feb. 2009.

6 Gilles Dorronsoro, "Focus and Exit: An Alternative Strategy for the Afghan War," Carnegie Endowment for International Peace, Jan. 2009 <carnegieendowment.org/ files/afghan_war-strategy.pdf>

7 Agence France-Presse, "Most Americans Oppose Afghanistan War: Poll," *Australian* 7 Aug. 2009 <www.theaustralian.news.com.au/story/0,25197,258953 98-12335,00.html>

8 Jonathan Weisman, "Poll Reflects Afghan War Doubts, *Wall Street Journal* 24 Sept. 2009 <online.wsj.com/article/SB125365402637131937.html>

9 Senate Armed Services Committee Reconfirmation Hearing, 15 Sept. 2009 <www.jcs.mil/speech.aspx?ID=1244>

10 Michael Moore and James Fussel, *Kunar and Nuristan*, Institute for the Study of War, July 2009. <www.understandingwar.org/files/Afghanistan_Report_1 .pdf>

11 See Kilcullen, *The Accidental Guerrilla: Fighting Small Wars in the Midst of a Big One* (New York: Oxford University Press, 2009), 103–104.

12 Jon Cohen and Jennifer Agiesta, "Poll of Afghans Shows Drop in Support for US Mission," *Washington Post* 10 Feb. 2009.

13 Paul Fitzgerald and Elizabeth Gould, *Invisible History: Afghanistan's Untold Story* (San Francisco: City Lights, 2009), 322.

14 Ibid., 316.

15 David Loyn, *In Afghanistan: Two Hundred Years of British, Russian and American Occupation* (New York: Palgrave Macmillan, 2009), 228.

16 Helen Duffy, "Responding to September 11: The Framework of International Law," INTERIGHTS (Lancaster House, London), Oct. 2001.

17 Ian S. Livingston, Heather Messera, and Jeremy Shapiro, Brookings Afghanistan Index, 12 Nov. 2009 <www.brookings.edu/foreign-policy/~/media/Files/Programs/FP/afghanistan%20index/index.pdf>

18 Helen Pidd, "Afghan Civilian Casualty Rate at Highest Since Taliban Rule," *Guardian* 17 Feb. 2009.

19 Associated Press, "Afghan Civilian Deaths Up 24%: UN," CBC Canada, 1 Aug. 2009 <www.cbc.ca/world/story/2009/07/31/afghan-civilian-deaths.html>

20 "Troops in Contact: Airstrikes and Civilian Deaths in Afghanistan," Human Rights Watch, 7 Sept. 2009 <www.hrw.org/en/news/2008/09/07/afghanistan-civilian-deaths-airstrikes>

21 Anand Gopal and Yochi J. Dreazen, "Afghan Civilians Hit, Straining US Alliance," *Wall Street Journal* 5 Sept. 2009 <online.wsj.com/article/SB125204283693185887.html>

22 ICasualties.org: Operation Enduring Freedom, 11 Nov. 2009 <icasualties.org/oef/>

23 Livingston, Messera, and Shapiro, Brookings Afghanistan Index, 12 Nov. 2009.

24 Remarks by Secretary Eric K. Shinseki, Office of Public and Intergovernmental Affairs, Department of Veterans Affairs, 26 Oct. 2009 <www1.va.gov/opa/speeches/2009/09_1026.asp>

25 MSNBC, "Wartime Brain Injuries Could Reach 360,000," 4 March 2009 <www.msnbc.msn.com/id/29513359/>

26 Fact Sheet, National Priorities Project, 9 Sept. 2009 <nationalpriorities.org/2009/09/02/quick-facts-US-military-operations-Afghanistan>

27 Amy Belasco, "The Cost of Iraq, Afghanistan and Other Global War on Terror Operations," Congressional Research Service, 15 May 2009 <www.fas.org/sgp/crs/natsec/RL33110.pdf>

28 National Priorities Project/AFSC, "The Cost of War in Afghanistan," April 2009 <www.nationalpriorities.org/auxiliary/costofwar/cost_of_war_afghanistan.pdf>

29 Sage Stossel, "The Battle Hymn of the Republic," *Atlantic* 18 Sept. 2001 <www.theatlantic.com/unbound/flashbks/battlehymn.htm>

30 CNN, "Transcript of President Bush's Address," 21 Sept. 2001 <archives.cnn.com/2001/US/09/20/gen.bush.transcript/>

31 Ibid.

32 Cost of War Counter, National Priorities Project, 12 Aug. 2009

33 Karen DeYoung and Greg Jaffe, "US Ambassador Seeks More Money for Afghanistan," *Washington Post* 12 Aug. 2009.

34 "Remarks of the President on a New Beginning," White House transcript, Cairo University, 4 June 2009.

35 Helene Cooper, "Military Says Afghan Force is Insufficient," *New York Times* 24 Aug. 2009.

36 August Cole, "US Adding Contractors at Fast-Pace" *Wall Street Journal* 24 Dec. 2009 <online.wsj.com/ article/SB125971465513072063.html>

37 Sheryl Gay Stolberg and Helene Cooper, "Obama Speeds Troops and Vows to Start Pullout in 2011," *New York Times* 2 Dec. 2009.

38 *Meet the Press*, MSNBC, 7 Dec. 2008 <www.msnbc.msn.com/id/28097635/page/3/>

39 "Prepared Remarks of President Barack Obama," White House transcript, 28 March 2009.

40 Karen DeYoung, "Afghan Conflict Will Be Reviewed," *Washington Post* 13 Jan. 2009.

41 Ibid.

42 "Prepared Remarks of President Barack Obama."

43 "Senate Confirmation Hearing for Secretary of State Nominee Hillary Clinton," the American Presidency Project, University of California–Santa Barbara, 13 Jan. 2009 <www.presidency.ucsb.edu/ws/ index.php?pid=85454>

44 DeYoung, "Afghan Conflict."

45 "Remarks of the President on a New Beginning."

46 Walter Pincus, "US Construction in Afghanistan Sign of Long Commitment," *Washington Post* 13 Jan. 2009.

47 *Morning Edition*, NPR, 10 Aug. 2009.

48 "US Commander Says Taliban Have Afghan Momentum," Reuters, 10 Aug. 2009 <www.newsdaily.com/stories/sp491178-us-afghanistan-taliban-general/>

49 Katherine Tiedeman, "Holbrooke on Success: We'll Know it When We See it," *Foreign Policy*, 12 Aug. 2009 <afpak.foreignpolicy.com/posts/2009/08/12/holbrooke_on_success_we_ll_know_it_when_we_see_it>

50 Sheryl Gay Stolberg, "Obama Defends Afghanistan as a 'War of Necessity,'" *New York Times* 18 Aug. 2009.

51 William Safire, "That Dog Won't Bark," *New York Times* 24 Feb. 2002.

52 Reuters, "Afghanistan Solution Will Need More than Military Force—Obama," IrishTimes.com, 17 Feb. 2009 <www.irishtimes.com/newspaper/breaking/2009/0217/breaking75.htm>

53 James P. Dorian, "Oil, Gas in FSU Central Asia, Northwestern China," *Oil & Gas Journal* 10 Sept. 2001.

54 Cited in Barry O'Kelly, "Prospect of Oil Riches Speeds the Wheels of War," *Business Post* (Ireland) 28 Oct. 2001.

55 Ibid.

56 As quoted in "How Oil Interests Play Out in US Bombing of Afghanistan," Drillbits and Tailings, Project Underground, 31 Oct. 2001 <www.moles.org/ProjectUnderground/drillbits/6_08/1.html>

57 O'Kelly, "Prospect of Oil Riches."

58 Ibid.

59 "Pipeline Politics: Oil, the Taliban and the Political Balance of Central Asia," WorldPress.org Special Report, Nov. 2001.

60 Cited in Laura Flanders, "Oil Omissions: Bush Sr., Cheney Have Big Stakes in Saudi Status Quo," WorkingforChange.com, 18 Oct. 2001.

61 Interview with Zbigniew Brzezinski, *Le Nouvelle Observateur* 15–21 Jan. 1998.

62 Steve Coll, *Ghost Wars: The Secret History of the CIA, Afghanistan, and Bin Laden from the Soviet Invasion to September 10, 2001* (New York: Penguin Books, 2004), 17.

63 Interview with Zbigniew Brzezinski.

64 Coll, 125.

65 Omid Marzban, "Gulbuddin Hekmatyar: From Holy Warrior to Wanted Terrorist," *Terrorist Monitor* 4.18, 21 Sept. 2006 <www.jamestown.org/programs/gta/single/?tx_ttnews%5Btt_news%5D=909&tx_ttnews%5BbackPid%5D=181&no_cache=1>

66 Eqbal Ahmad, "Terrorism: Theirs and Ours," *The

Selected Writings of Eqbal Ahmad (New York: Columbia University Press, 2006), 258.

67 CNN, "US Missiles Pound Targets in Afghanistan, Sudan," 20 Aug. 1998.

68 Zalmay Khalilzad, "Afghanistan: Time to Reengage," *Washington Post* 7 Oct. 1996.

69 Joe Stephens and David B. Ottaway, "Afghan Roots Keep Adviser Firmly in the Inner Circle: Consultant's Policy Influence Goes Back to Reagan Era," *Washington Post* 23 Nov. 2001.

70 "Pipeline Politics: Oil, The Taliban and the Political Balance of Central Asia," WorldPress.org Special Report, Nov. 2001 <www.worldpress.org/specials/pp/front.htm>

71 Juan Cole, "Hekmatyar Goes Al-Qaeda," 6 May 2006 <www.juancole.com/2006/05/hekmatyar-goes-al-qaeda-kabul-bomb.html>

72 David Rohde and David E. Sanger, "How a 'Good' War in Afghanistan Went Bad," *New York Times* 12 Aug. 2007 <www.nytimes.com/2007/08/12/world/asia/12afghan.html>

73 Sarah Ladbury, "Testing Hypotheses on Radicalisation in Afghanistan: Why Do Men Join the Taliban and Hizb-I Islami? How Much do Local Communities Support Them?" Department of International Development report (August 2009), 23.

74 "Maktab al-Khidamat," GlobalSecurity.org <www.globalsecurity.org/security/profiles/maktab_al-khidamat.htm>

75 CNN, "US Missiles Pound Targets in Afghanistan, Sudan," 20 Aug. 1998 <www.cnn.com/US/9808/20/us.strikes.01/>

76 Rohde and Sanger, "How a 'Good' War in Afghanistan Went Bad."

77 Peter Bergen, "Ahmad Shah Massoud," *Time* 6 Oct.

2006 <www.time.com/time/asia/2006/heroes/nb_ massoud. html>

78 Final Report of the National Commission on Terrorist Attacks Upon the United States <www.9-11 commission.gov/report/911Report_Exec.htm> 20 Sept. 2004.

79 Report of the Special Inspector General for Afghanistan Reconstruction, April 2009 <www.sigar.mil/ reports/quarterlyreports/Apr09/pdf/Report_April_2009 .pdf>

80 "Sustainable Security in Afghanistan: Crafting an Effective and Responsible Strategy for the Forgotten Front," Center for American Progress (March 2009), 10.

81 Thom Shanker and Eric Schmitt, "US Plans Vastly Expanded Afghan Security Force," *New York Times* 18 March 2009.

82 McChrystal, Commander's Initial Assessment, 30 August 2009, 2–15 <media.washingtonpost.com/wp-srv/ politics/documents/Assessment_Redacted_092109.pdf>

83 Kilcullen, *The Accidental Guerrilla*, 107–109.

84 "Text of Colonel Reese's Memo," *New York Times* 31 July 2009 <www.nytimes.com/2009/07/31/world/ middleeast/31advtext.html?scp=1&sq=Reese%20memo&s t=cse>

85 Paul R. Pillar, "Who's Afraid of a Terrorist Haven?" *Washington Post* 16 Sept. 2009.

86 Gilles Dorronsoro, "Focus and Exit."

87 Lindsey Graham, Joseph I. Lieberman, and John McCain, "Only Decisive Force Can Prevail in Afghanistan," *Wall Street Journal* 14 Sept. 2009.

88 International Council on Security and Development, Afghanistan map <www.icosmaps.net>

89 See Ladbury, "Testing Hypotheses on Radicali- sation," 14, for characteristics attributed to both good and bad Taliban.

90 Thomas Ruttig, "The Other Side—Dimensions of the Afghan Insurgency: Causes, Actors and Approaches to 'Talks,'" Afghanistan Analysts Network, July 2009.

91 Atiq Sarwari and Robert Crews, "Epilogue: Afghanistan and the Pax Americana," in *The Taliban and the Crisis of Afghanistan* (Cambridge: Harvard University Press, 2008), 315–316.

92 As quoted in Antonio Donini, "Afghanistan: Humanitarianism under Threat" (Feinstein International Center, Tufts University, March 2009), 4.

93 "Silence is Violence: End the Abuse of Women in Afghanistan," United Nations Assistance Mission in Afghanistan (UNAMA) and Office of the High Commissioner for Human Rights (OHCHR) (Kabul), 8 July 2009, 28.

94 Oxfam, "Smart Development in Practice: Field Report from Afghanistan" (2009), 5.

95 Reuters, "Maternal Mortality Rate High in Afghanistan: UN," 26 Jan. 2009 <in.reuters.com/article/domesticNews/idINISL40747920090126>

96 UNDP, "Gender-Related Development Index," Human Development Report 2009 <hdr.undp.org/en/media/HDR_2009_EN_Table_J.pdf>

97 Sonali Kolhatkar and Mariam Rawi, "Why is a Leading Feminist Organization Lending its Name to Support Escalation in Afghanistan?" posted 8 July 2009 at www.alternet.org

98 UNDP, "Gender-Related Development Index."

99 Marc Erikson, "Mr. Karzai Goes to Washington," *Asia Times* 29 Jan. 2002 <www.atimes.com/c-asia/DA29Ag02.html>

100 "Interview: Lakhdar Brahimi," *Frontline*, PBS, 4 May 2002 <www.pbs.org/wgbh/pages/frontline/shows/campaign/interviews/brahimi.html>

101 Joshua Partlow and Karen DeYoung, "With Karzai Favored to Win, US Walks a Fine Line," *Washington Post* 14

Aug. 2009.

102 "Tallies Cost of War," National Priorities Project, 16 July 2009 <www.nationalpriorities.org/newsletter/ 2009/07/16/Cost-of-War-Tops-$915-Billion>

103 "Losing Afghanistan?" *Economist* 22 Aug. 2009.

104 Atif B, "Phantom at the Polls," *New York Times* 18 Aug. 2009.

105 Hassina Sherjan, "Apathy Among the Educated," *New York Times* 18 Aug. 2009.

106 Deborah Zabarenko, "US Offers Lesson on How to Tell Cluster Bombs from Food Packs," Reuters, *Washington Post* 30 Oct. 2001.

107 Steven Mufson, "Pentagon Changing Color of Airdropped Meals," *Washington Post* 2 Nov. 2001.

108 Kilcullen, *The Accidental Guerrilla*, 102.

109 The Code of Conduct for the International Red Cross and Red Crescent Movement and NGOs in Disaster Relief (Geneva: ICRC, 1994) <www.icrc.org/web/eng/ siteeng0.nsf/htmlall/code-of-conduct-290296>

110 ACBAR bulletin obtained 27 Dec. 2002, quoted by Christopher Holshek in Kevin M. Cahill, ed., *The Pulse of Humanitarian Assistance* (New York: Fordham University Press, 2007), 110.

111 Bonnie Malkin, "Al-Qaeda Plots to Kidnap Civilian Workers in Afghanistan," *Telegraph* (London) 16 Sept. 2009.

112 Vanessa M. Gezari, "Rough Terrain," *Washington Post* magazine 30 Aug. 2009.

113 See for example, "Shinwar to Dur Baba Road Construction Project, Nangarhar, Afghanistan— Environmental Assessment," prepared by USAID/Kabul and International Relief and Development, 19 Nov. 2008 <pdf.usaid.gov/pdf_docs/PNADN169.pdf>

114 Patrick Fruchet and Mike Kendellen. "Landmine Impact Survey of Afghanistan: Results and Implications for

Planning," *Journal of Mine Action* 7 March 2006
<maic.jmu.edu/journal/9.2/focus/fruchet/fruchet.htm>

115 USDA, "Agriculture in Afghanistan: Rebuilding
for a Stable, Secure Country" <www.fas.usda.gov/
country/Afghanistan/us-afghanistan.asp>

116 "Afghanistan: UN Humanitarian Action Plan Mid-
Year Review, 2009," 7 <ochadms.unog.ch/quickplace/
cap/main.nsf/h_Index/MYR_2009_Afghanistan_HAP/$F
ILE/MYR_2009_Afghanistan_HAP_SCREEN.pdf?OpenEl
ement>

117 Fred Pearce, "The Wasteland: Afghanistan Will
Remain Scarred by War Long after the Bombing Stops," *New
Scientist* 173.2324 (5 Jan. 2002): 4(1). Academic OneFile.
Gale. Duke University Library–Perkins. 30 July 2009
<proxy.lib.duke.edu:2087/itx/start.do?prodId=AONE>

118 UN Environment Program, "Afghanistan's
Environment 2008," 16 <www.reliefweb.int/rw/
RWFiles2008.nsf/FilesByRWDocUnidFilename/JBRN-
7QEJD5-full_report.pdf/$File/full_report.pdf>

119 UN Report, "The Situation in Afghanistan and its
Implications for International Peace and Security"
A/63/892-S/2009/323, 11.

120 Gretchen Peters, *Seeds of Terror: How Heroin is
Bankrolling the Taliban and Al Qaeda* (New York: St. Martin's
Press, 2009), 237.

121 David Mansfield and Adam Pain, "Counter-
Narcotics in Afghanistan: The Failure of Success?" Afghanistan Research and Evaluation Unit (AREU) (Dec. 2008), 3.

122 Ibid., 16.

123 Gareth Porter, "US Choice Hardly McChrystal
Clear," *Asia Times* 14 May 2009.

124 Ibid.

125 Richard Sale, "A New Kind of War Part 1," Sic
Semper Tyrannis (blog), 25 May 2009
<turcopolier.typepad.com/sic_semper_tyrannis/2009/05

/a-new-kind-of-war-part-1-richard-sale.html#more>

126 Donald M. Snow, "Will COIN Work in Afghanistan?" *New Atlanticist* 20 July 2009.

127 "US Rejects Taliban Offer to Try bin Laden," CNN, 7 Oct. 2001 <archives.cnn.com/2001/US/10/07/ret.us.taliban/>

128 "Fighting on Two Fronts: A Chronology," *Frontline*, PBS (online) <www.pbs.org/wgbh/pages/frontline/shows/campaign/etc/cron.html>

129 "Interview: Lakhdar Brahimi," *Frontline*.

130 NATO, "NATO's Role in Afghanistan," 27 May 2009 <www.nato.int/issues/Afghanistan/index.html>

131 Timo Noetzel and Sibylle Scheipers, "The Alliance and the Limits of Its Strategy," German Institute for International and Security Affairs, 2007 <www.qantara.de/webcom/show_article.php/_c-476/_nr-839/i.html>

132 Mark McDonald, "China Trains Afghans and Iraqis to Clear Mines," *New York Times* 16 Sept. 2009.

133 Thomas Friedman, "The End of NATO?" *New York Times* 3 Feb. 2002.

134 *Morning Edition*, NPR, 21 Sept. 2009.

135 Barbara Crossette, "Lakhdar Brahimi: Afghanistan's Future," *Nation* 9 March 2009.

136 Thomas Friedman, "Noblesse Oblige," *New York Times* 31 July 2001.

137 Crossette, "Lakhdar Brahimi."

138 "Blast Hits Kabul UN Compound," BBC, 30 March 2003 <news.bbc.co.uk/2/hi/south_asia/2901421.stm>

139 Moin Ansari, "Where Did the $10 Billion in Aid to Pakistan Go?" Pakistan Defence Forum, 27 July 2009 <www.defence.pk/forums/economy-development/30821-where-did-10-billion-us-aid-pakistan-go.html>

140 Graham Usher, "The Afghan Triangle: Kashmir, India, Pakistan," *Middle East Report* (Summer 2009).

141 Declan Walsh, "Air Strike Kills Taliban Leader Baitullah Mehsud," *Guardian* 7 Aug. 2009.

142 Owen Fay, "Pakistanis See US as Biggest Threat," al-Jazeera, 13 Aug. 2009 <english.aljazeera.net/news/asia/2009/08/20098910857878664.html>

143 Jane Perlez and Pir Zubair Shah, "Pakistan Army Said to Be Linked to Swat Killings," *New York Times* 14 Sept. 2009.

144 Graham Usher, "The Afghan Triangle."

145 Owen Fay, "Pakistanis See US as Biggest Threat."

146 CIA Factbook, "Country Comparison, GDP" (2008 est.) <www.cia.gov/library/publications/the-world-factbook/rankorder/2004rank.html?countryName=Pakistan&countryCode=pk&regionCode=sas&rank=173#pk>

147 CNN, "Iranian President Condemns September 11 Attacks," 12 Nov. 2001 <archives.cnn.com/2001/WORLD/meast/11/12/khatami.interview.cnna/index.html>

148 James Dobbins, "How to Talk to Iran," *Washington Post* (online) 22 July 2007 <www.rand.org/commentary/2007/07/22/WP.html>

149 Barbara Slavin, "Iran Helped Overthrow Taliban, Candidate Says," *USA Today* 9 June 2005 <www.usatoday.com/news/world/2005-06-09-iran-taliban_x.htm>

150 Afzal Khan, "Trade Between Afghanistan and Iran Reaches Record Levels," *Eurasia Daily Monitor* 8 July 2004 <www.jamestown.org/single/?no_cache=1&tx_ttnews%5Btt_news%5D=30077>

151 Golnaz Esfandiari, "Afghanistan/Iran: Relations Between Tehran, Kabul Growing Stronger," Radio Free Europe/Radio Liberty, 26 Jan. 2005 <www.parstimes.com/news/archive/2005/rfe/afghanistan_iran_relations.html>

152 Christina Lamb, "US and Iran Open Afghanistan Peace Talks," *Sunday Times* (London) 29 March 2009

<www.timesonline.co.uk/tol/news/world/middle_east/a
rticle5993094.ece>

153 General Petraeus, from his new counterinsurgency manual, as quoted in Loyn, *In Afghanistan*, 226.

154 Eric Schmitt, "In a General's Grim Assessment of
Afghanistan, a Catalyst for Obama," *New York Times* 22 Sept.
2009.

155 McChrystal, Commander's Initial Assessment, 2–9.

156 George Will, "Time to Get Out of Afghanistan,"
Washington Post 1 Sept. 2009.

157 Leslie Gelb, "How to Leave Afghanistan," *New York
Times* 13 March 2009.

158 Associated Press, "General: US Troops Must
Protect Afghans," MSNBC, 24 June 2009 <www.msnbc.
msn.com/id/31530822>

159 Thom Shanker, "Message to Muslim World Gets a
Pentagon Critique," *New York Times* 28 Aug. 2009.

160 Eyal Weizman, "Walking Through Walls,"
European Institute for Progressive Cultural Policies, Jan.
2007 <eipcp.net/transversal/0507/weizman/en>

161 Scott Wilson and Al Kamen, "'Global War On
Terror' Is Given New Name," *Washington Post* 25 March 2009.

162 Thom Shanker, "US Military to Stay in
Philippines," *New York Times* 20 Aug. 2009.

163 Editorial, "Losing Afghanistan?" *Economist* 22 Aug.
2009 < www.economist.com/opinion/
displaystory.cfm?story_id=14258750>

164 Dorronsoro, "Focus and Exit."

165 Fitzgerald and Gould, *Invisible History*, 324.

166 Shanker, "Message to Muslim World."

167 AP, "In Basra, Violence is a Tenth of What it was
Before British Pullback, General Says," 15 Nov. 2007.

168 George Friedman, "Strategic Divergence: The War
Against the Taliban and the War Against Al Qaeda," Stratfor
Global Intelligence, 26 Jan. 2009 < www.stratfor.com/

weekly/20090126_strategic_divergence_war_against_talib
an_and_war_against_al_qaeda>

169 Editorial, "Losing Afghanistan?" *Economist*.

170 ABC/BBC/ARD Poll, "Support for US Efforts Plummets Amid Afghanistan's Ongoing Strife," 9 Feb. 2009 <http://news.bbc.co.uk/2/shared/bsp/hi/pdfs/05_02_0 9afghan_poll_2009.pdf>

171 George Will, "Time to Get Out of Afghanistan," *Washington Post* 1 Sept. 2009.

172 Andrew Bacevich, "Is the Afghanistan War Worth Fighting?" *Washington Post* 31 Aug. 2009.

173 Elisabeth Bumiller and Mark Landler, "US Afghan Envoy Urges Caution on Troop Increase," *New York Times* 12 Nov. 2009.

RESOURCES

Books

Ali, Tariq. *The Duel: Pakistan on the Flight Path of American Power*. New York: Scribner, 2008.

Ahmad, Eqbal. *The Selected Writings of Eqbal Ahmad*. New York: Columbia University Press, 2006.

Ahmad, Eqbal, with David Barsamian. *Confronting Empire*. Boston: South End Press, 2000.

Bennis, Phyllis. *Before and After: US Foreign Policy and the War on Terrorism*. Northampton: Olive Branch Press, 2002.

————. *Challenging Empire: How People, Governments, and the UN Defy US Power*. Northampton: Olive Branch Press, 2006.

Bick, Barbara. *Walking the Precipice: Witness to the Rise of the Taliban in Afghanistan*. New York: The Feminist Press at CUNY, 2009.

Chomsky, Noam. *Pirates and Emperors, Old and New: International Terrorism in the Real World*. London: Pluto Press, 2002.

Coll, Steve. *Ghost Wars: The Secret History of the CIA, Afghanistan and Bin Laden from the Soviet Invasion to September 10, 2001*. New York: Penguin Books, 2004.

Cooley, John K. *Unholy Wars: Afghanistan, America and International Terrorism*. London: Pluto Press, 1999.

Crews, Robert D., and Amin Tarzi, eds. *The Taliban and the Crisis of Afghanistan*. Cambridge: Harvard University Press, 2008.

Dreyfuss, Robert. *Devil's Game: How the United States Helped Unleash Fundamentalist Islam*. New York: Henry Holt & Co., 2005.

Fitzgerald, Paul, and Elizabeth Gould. *Invisible History: Afghanistan's Untold Story*. San Francisco: City Lights, 2009.

Hersh, Seymour. *Chain of Command: The Road from 9/11 to Abu Ghraib*. New York: HarperCollins, 2004.

Johnson, Chalmers. *Nemesis: The Last Days of the American Republic*. New York: Metropolitan Books, 2006.

Juhasz, Antonia. *The Tyranny of Oil: The World's Most Powerful Industry—And What We Must Do to Stop It*. New York: HarperCollins, 2008.

Kolhatkar, Sonali, and James Ingalls. *Bleeding Afghanistan: Washington, Warlords, and the Propaganda of Silence*. New York: Seven Stories Press, 2006.

Loyn, David. *In Afghanistan: Two Hundred Years of British, Russian and American Occupation*. New York: Palgrave Macmillan, 2009.

Mamdani, Mahmood. *Good Muslim, Bad Muslim: America, the Cold War and the Roots of Terror*. New York: Doubleday, 2004.

Mayer, Jane. *The Dark Side: The Inside Story of How the War on Terror Turned into a War on American Ideals*. New York: Doubleday, 2008.

Newell, Richard S. *The Politics of Afghanistan*. Ithaca: Cornell University Press, 1972.

Peters, Gretchen. *Seeds of Terror: How Heroin is Bankrolling the Taliban and al Qaeda*. New York: St. Martin's Press, 2009.

Rashid, Ahmed. *Taliban: Militant Islam, Oil and Fundamentalism in Central Asia*. New Haven: Yale University Press, 2001.

———. *Descent into Chaos: The United States and the Failure of Nation Building in Pakistan, Afghanistan, and Central Asia*. New York: Viking, 2008.

Semple, Michael. *Negotiating with the Taliban: Reconciliation in Afghanistan and Pakistan?* Washington, DC: US Institute of Peace, 2009.

News, Analysis, and Resources
Afghanistan Analysts Network (independent policy analysis, www.aan-afghanistan.com)

American Friends Service Committee (fact sheets, speakers, www.afsc.org)

Brookings Afghanistan Index (overall statistics, www.brookings.edu/foreign-policy/afghanistan-index.aspx)

Icasualties (documents, casualty statistics, www.icasualties.org)

Institute for Policy Studies (primers, fact sheets, speakers, www.ips-dc.org)

National Priorities Project (military budget analysis, www.nationalpriorities.org)

Rethink Afghanistan (short videos opposing the war, www.rethinkafghanistan.com)

Revolutionary Association of the Women of Afghanistan (news, speakers, www.rawa.org)

Organizations Taking Action against the War
9/11 Families for Peaceful Tomorrows
    (www.peacefultomorrows.org)
Code Pink (www.codepink4peace.org)
Iraq Veterans Against the War (www.ivaw.org)
Military Families Speak Out (www.mfso.org)
Peace Action (www.peace-action.org)
United for Peace and Justice Afghanistan working group
    (www.unitedforpeace.org)
US Labor Against the War (www.uslaboragainstwar.org)
Veterans for Peace (www.veteransforpeace.org)
Win Without War (www.winwithoutwarus.org)